For Miss Anne M. Smith.

Welcome to Keio University

Eiichi Kiyooka

September 11, 1953

JAPANESE IN
THIRTY HOURS

Naka-yoshi

(P. 118)

JAPANESE
IN
THIRTY HOURS

FIRST COURSE IN JAPANESE LANGUAGE FOR
EITHER CLASS ROOM USE OR FOR SELF STUDY

Systematized Direct Method

by

EIICHI KIYOOKA

Professor at Keio University,
One time Instructor at Columbia University and
Visiting Professor at University of Hawaii

TOKYO
THE HOKUSEIDO PRESS

FOREWORD

These lessons in Japanese language were first developed while the author was an instructor of Japanese language and history at Columbia University Extention. Later they were published in serial form in the Japanese-American of New York City.

At the university the time allotted was only two hours a week and the students, who were mostly adults already in business, usually gave up the lessons after one semester, because they were learning the language in a hurry for business or for travels. Therefore the total number of hours available for instruction were no more than thirty hours, a semester being fifteen weeks. Under these conditions the instructor was obliged to develop a very efficient system of instruction which covered the entire field of the Japanese language with all the superfluity eliminated.

The Method The basic idea of this method is to classify all the expressions into types and to teach one type with its variations in each lesson, the variation being made by simple substitution of words. After all the types have been covered, a student—theoretically—will be able to express any idea in Japanese if he is provided with necessary words. And the words may be obtained from a dictionary.

A student is advised to first look over the table of

contents thoroughly to see what variety of things he is to learn in this book.

The Lessons Every lesson in this volume is patterned after a uniform order. The *Example* is always given at the beginning, then the *Key Words*, *Vocabulary*, and *Exercises*. The *Example* serves as the model sentence. A student is expected to memorize it and also to learn to form different sentences of the same type by substitution of words. The *Key Words* are the uninterchangeable words in the *Example*. With the key words and vocabulary any number of sentences can be formed. A student should form many more sentences for himself than are found in the *Exercises*.

Each lesson will widen the scope of Japanese language. As the scope widens, a student should make use of it in actual conversation with a Japanese in so much the wider field of talk.

Any number of lessons may be taught together in one hour according to the circumstances and the ability of the student. At Columbia an average student found no difficulty in finishing the whole course in thirty hours. In fact the author has a record of having finished them in twelve hours with a special student. However, as the lessons are somewhat enlarged in this book, it will be advisable to allow a few more hours than exactly thirty for average students.

Usually the first three lessons are taken up together on the first hour. And it is a never failing thrill to an instructor to see the happy expressions of his pupils when they find themselves conversing in full sentences from the very first hour—" Is this a book ? " " Yes, that is a book." " No, that is not a book." Etc.

After all, the language acquirement is a matter of practice. There should be ninety-five percent of drill and five percent of instruction and theorizing.

Vocabulary An average man cannot learn and master more than five or six words a day unless he makes the language study his chief concern. Too many words are more confusing than helpful. Therefore the vocabulary in these lessons has been kept down to the minimum. Words should be picked up from a dictionary whenever necessity arises. One should not be too ambitious about vocabulary. Learning sentence construction is much more important.

One interesting endeavour made in these lessons is the use of the foreign words in Japanese such as " table," " knife," " fork," and " note book." There are some six hundred of them in daily use—an unexpectedly large number until one makes a thorough investigation. Their pronunciation may be quite twisted, but they are very easy for foreigners to learn.

Pronunciation and Spelling In Japanese there are five vowel sounds :

    a   approximately as the *a* in " mat "
    i   approximately as the *i* in " big "
    u   approximately as the *u* in " put "
    e   approximately as the *e* in " bed "
    o   approximately as the *o* in " soft "

Also, there are long vowel sounds, as in English, which have twice the value of the short vowel sounds listed above. For instance, the *a* in *father* is a long *a*; the *o* in *note* is a long *o*. In Japanese the long sound is indicated by either repeating the vowels as **Tookyoo** and **juu** (ten) or by a mark over the vowels as **Tōkyō**. Newspapers and books in general are often careless about indicating the long sounds and print **Tokyo** as if it were a two syllable word though it is pronounced as a four syllable word. **Yokohama** also is a four syllable word, for each of its syllables is short.

The use of the consonants is practically the same as in English, for, indeed, the Romanized system of Japanese spelling employed in this book was first organized by Dr. J. C. Hepburn on the basis of English usage in the early days. In recent years what is called the Japanese System of Romaji was created, but the old Hepburn system is prefered because it offers a much easier approach for the foreigners and also it gives a better start for the Japanese in their study of English. Both systems along with Kana (the Japanese syllabary or letters) are explained more fully in the Appendices.

After all, pronunciation cannot be explained on paper. It is much better to have a teacher or friend demonstrate it.

Accent The accent in Japanese language is slight and unimportant. In most cases a wrong use of it will not make a speech ambiguous. And so, it is not touched upon in the lessons of this volume. However, it should be learned with care along with the pronunciation as it is one of the indicators of skill in the language.

One hint I wish to give here is that the Japanese accent is mainly "pitch accent" and not the "stress accent" as in English. Without this knowledge one may have to go through a long and puzzling struggle before grasping it.

Japanese is Easy for a Beginner Polite expressions, lady's way of speaking, and such subtleties which make the Japanese language one of the richest in the world have been carefully avoided in the lessons of this volume. Only one kind of expressions which are presentable enough for any one, but not too colloquial for foreigners, are given. In that one kind, the author believes, practically all the basic and necessary expressions have been covered. Therefore, at the end of the course a student is expected to be able to express any thought in Japanese with the aid of a dictionary.

Japanese is one of the richest languages in the world. Naturally the full mastery of its elegant uses is very difficult even for a native. However, the grammar of the spoken Japanese is very simple. For a beginner learning to speak it for daily purposes, the Japanese should be easier than any other language, which I trust the following lessons will prove.

Summer, 1949.

Tokyo.   EIICHI KIYOOKA

CONTENTS

Dec 15

JAPANESE IN THIRTY HOURS

LESSON 1

Sentences of the type "This is a book."

Example:

Kore-wa hon-de su.   *{ This is a book.*
  | | | *{ These are books.*
 this   book   is

The Japanese language has no article. Also the number, gender and person are, for the most part, left unregard ed. **Hon** may be one book or several books. One verb form serves for *is, are,* or *am.*

Whenever there is **-wa**, it is safe to assume that the preceding word or phrase is the subject of the sentence. In the same way **-de** usually denotes a predicate complement.

The full form of the word for *is, are,* or *am* is **ari-masu,** but in actual usage it is usually abbreviated to the mere last syllable **su.** (See Lesson 3, Negation.) In a formal speech the full form may be used:—**Kore-wa hon-de ari-masu.** But that is beyond our scope for the present.

The word order in a sentence is usually—the subject first, the verb last, and the predicate complement or the object between.

Key Words:

-wa	word-ending for subject
-de	word-ending for predicate complement[1]
su (ari-masu)	*is, are, am*

Key Words are the essential frame-work which is always used in forming sentences of the same type.

Substituting **sore** in place of **Kore**, we have:—

Sore-wa hon-de su.   { *That is a book.*
| | | | { *Those are books.*
that   book   is

Because the person is unregarded in Japanese, " I am a man " is a sentence of the same type.

Watakushi-wa otoko-de su.   *I am a man.*
  | | |
I   man   is

Thus any number of sentences may be formed upon the frame-work of the key words.

Let us see what Exercises we can have with the five words of the Vocabulary.

Vocabulary:

kore	*this, these*
sore	*that, those*

---

[1] According to the regular Japanese grammar **-wa** and **-de** are called **Tenioha** or post-positions (in analogy to the English prepositions) and they are treated as independent words. However, from class room experiences I have decided to treat them as endings, because a foreign student is very liable to forget them as too insignificant unless they are attached securely to the preceding word with a hyphen.

hon	*book, books*
watakushi	*I, myself*
otoko	*man, men*

Exercises:

Kore-wa hon-de su.	This is a book. These are books.
Kore-wa watakushi-de su.	This is myself.
Kore-wa otoko-de su.	This is a man. These are men.
Sore-wa hon-de su.	That is a book. Those are books.
Sore-wa watakushi-de su	That is myself.
Sore-wa otoko-de su.	That is a man. Those are men.
Watakushi-wa otoko-de su.	I am a man.
Watakushi-wa sore-de su.	I am that.

LESSON 2

Interrogation: " Is this a book ? "

Example

Kore-wa hon-de su ka ?
  | | | |
 this   book   is ?

Is this a book ?
Are these books ?

An interrogative sentence is formed by the simple addition of **ka** at the end. The order of the words is not changed. This **ka** will turn any sentence interrogative —not only simple sentences but long, complicated ones.

Kore-wa nan'-de su ka?

  | | | |
this   what   is ?

{ *What is this?*
{ *What are these?*

Nan' is an abbreviation of **nani** (*what*). So, note that a word like *what* (or *who* and *where*) is placed at the usual position in a sentence, which makes the Japanese language much simpler than English.

Key Words:

    -wa   word-ending for subject

    -de   word-ending for predicate complement

   su (**ari-masu**)   *is, are, am*

    ka   **?**

Vocabulary:

      hai   *yes*

      nan' (**nani**)   *what?*

      anata   *you*

      " naifu " (an English word) *knife, knives*

Exercises:

Kore-wa hon-de su ka?	{ Is this a book? { Are these book?
Hai, sore-wa hon-de su.	{ Yes, that is a book. { Yes, those are books.
Sore-wa anata-de su ka?	Is that you?
Hai, sore-wa watakushi-de su.	Yes, that is myself.
Anata-wa otoko-de su ka?	Are you a man?
Hai, watakushi-wa otoko-de su.	Yes, I am a man
Sore-wa naifu-de su ka?	{ Is that a knife? { Are those knives?

Hai, kore-wa naifu-de su.	{Yes, this is a knife. {Yes, these are knives.
Kore-wa nan'-de su ka?	{What is this? {What are these?
Sore-wa hon-de su.	{That is a book. {Those are books.
Sore-wa nan'-de su ka?	{What is that? {What are those?
Sore-wa naifu-de su.	{That is a knife. {Those are knives.
Anata-wa nan'-de su ka?	What are you?
Watakushi-wa otoko-de su.	I am a man.
Watakushi-wa nan'-de su ka?	What am I?
Anata-wa otoko-de su.	You are a man.

LESSON 3

Negation: "This is not a book."

Example:

Kore-wa hon-de ari-masen.   {*This is not a book.*
  | | | {*These are not books.*
this   book   is not

In negation the full form of the verb is used, because **ari-masen** has no abbreviated form.

To explain more fully, **ari** is the verb *to be* and **masu** is an auxiliary verb which has a usage analogous to that of the English *do*. This **masu** may be used after any verb, and the negation, past and future tenses, etc. can be formed by its inflexion. Therefore, learning the inflexion of **masu** alone will enable one to make use of all verbs in simple expressions

Kore-wa hon-de ari-masen ka ?   *Isn't this a book?*
The above usage of interrogation in negative form is exactly the same as in English. It implies that the speaker thinks that it is a book.

Key Words :

-wa	word-ending for subject
-de	word-ending for predicate complement
ari-masen	*is not, are not, am not*

Vocabulary :

" **fooku** " (English word)	*fork*
iie	*no*
-san	*Mr., Mrs., Miss* (Used after names. Here again we see that the Japanese language leaves gender unregarded)
soo	*so*
Soo-de su	*That is so* (contraction of **sore-wa soo-de su**)
Soo-de ari-masen	*That is not so* (contraction of **sore-wa soo-de ari-masen.**)
Soo-de su ka ?	*Is that so ?*

Exercises :

Sore-wa hon-de su ka ?	{Is that a book ? {Are those books ?
Iie, kore-wa hon-de ari-masen	{No, this is not a book. {No, these are not books.

Sore-wa fooku-de su ka?	{Is that a fork? {Are those forks?
Iie, sore-wa fooku-de ari-masen.	No, that is not a fork. (Also plural)
Sore-wa naifu-de su.	That is a knife. (Also plural)
Anata-wa Smith-san-de su ka?	Are you Mr. Smith? (Or Miss or Mrs.)
Iie, watakushi-wa Smith-de ari-masen.	No, I am not Smith.[1]
Anata-wa Kiyooka-san-de su ka?	Are you Mr. Kiyooka? (Or Miss, Mrs.)
Hai, soo-de su.	Yes, I am.
Anata-wa Smith-san-de ari-masen ka?	Aren't you Mr. Smith?
Iie, watakushi-wa Smith-de ari-masen.	No, I am not Smith.
Iie, soo-de ari-masen. Watakushi-wa Johnson-de su.	No, I am not. (No, that is not so.) I am Johnson.
Soo-de su ka?	Is that so?
Kore-wa nan'-de su ka? Kore-wa naifu-de su ka?	What is this? Is this a knife?
Hai, soo-de su.	Yes, it is.
Anata-wa otoko-de su ka?	Are you a man?
Iie, soo-de ari-masen.	No, I am not.
Soo-de su ka!	Is that so!

---

[1] Never say, "Watakushi-wa Smith-san-de ari-masen (or -de su.)" -San is a term of respect and it must not be used for the speaker himself. On this point -san is not an equivalent of *Mr.*, for one may say, "I am Mr. Smith."

LESSON 4

Possessive: "My book"

Examples .

Kore-wa watakushi-no hon-de su.

| | | |
| this | my | book   is |

> *This is my book.*
> *These are my books.*

Kore-wa watakushi-no-de su.

| | | |
| this | mine | is |

> *This is mine.*
> *These are mine.*

Kore-wa hako-no futa-de su.

| | | |
| this | box's | lid   is |

> *This is the lid of the box.*
> *These are the lids of the boxes.*

Kore-wa hako-no-de su.

> *This is box's.*   (and plural)

The use of **-no** serves for both *my* and *mine*. And the same usage of **-no** can be applied to things as well as to persons, as **Kore-wa hako-no-de su,** which has no corresponding expression in English.

Complete sentences are used in illustrating the use of possessive, because it is important that a student should learn the use of words in relation to the sentence. One should learn the whole sentence as a unit. It is not

enough to know **hako-no futa**; one must be able to say
"**Kore-wa hako-no-futa-de su**" in one breath.

Key Words:

> **-no**   *'s, (of)*

Vocabulary:

donata	*who?* (interrogative pronoun)
hako	*box, boxes*
futa	*lid, lids*
to	*and*
"**pen**"	*pen*
"**inku**"	*ink*
kimono	*clothes, dress*

Exercises:

Kore-wa anata-no hako-de su ka?	Is this your box?
Iie, sore-wa watakushi-no de ari-masen.	No, that is not mine.
Kore-wa hako-no futa-de su ka?	Is this the lid of a box?
Hai, soo-de su.	Yes, it is.
Kore-wa donata-no hako-de su ka?	Whose box is this?
Sore-wa watakushi-no hako-de su	That is my box.
Sore-wa donata-no-de su ka?	Whose is that?
Kore-wa Smith-san-no-de su	This is Smith's.

Kore-wa anata-no pen to inku-de su ka?	Are these your pen and ink?
Soo-de su, sore-wa watakushi-no-de su.	Yes, those are mine.
Sore-wa nan'-de su ka?	What is that?
Kore-wa Smith-san-no kimo-no-de su.	This is Smith's clothes.
Kore-wa pen-no hako-de su.	This is a box for the pen.
Kore-wa pen to inku-no hako-de su.	This is a box for the pen and ink.
Kore-wa pen-no hako-no futa-de su.	This is the lid of the box for the pen.
Kore-wa pen to inku-no hako-no futa-de su.	This is the lid of the box for the pen and ink.
Anata-no hako-wa kore-de su ka?	Is your box this?
Hai, watakushi-no hako-wa kore-de su.	Yes, my box is this.
Anata-no-wa kore-de su ka?	Is yours this?
Soo-de su, watakushi-no-wa kore-de su.[1]	Yes, mine is this.[1]

---

[1] In the above Exercises and in the subsequent Exercises the translations for plural have been left out for the sake of simplicity.

LESSON 5

Adjectives (1): "A good book"

Example:

Kore-wa yoi hon-de su.   *This is a good book.*
| this   good   book   is | *(and plural)*

In Japanese there are two kinds of adjectives—regular adjectives and noun-adjectives. The regular adjectives, which are studied in this lesson, and the verbs are the two parts of speech which have inflexions. Those inflexions will be taken up later, but it is well to notice now that the regular adjectives always end in i when used before nouns.

Vocabulary:

yoi	*good*
warui	*bad*
ookii	*big*
chiisai	*small*
donna	*what kind of?* (*donna* is a noun-adjective, because it ends in **na**)
" **hankachi** "	*handkerchief*
" **teeburu** "	*table*

Exercises:

Kore-wa yoi hon-de su ka?	Is this a good book?
Soo-de su, sore-wa yoi hon-de su	Yes, that is a good book.
Iie, sore-wa yoi hon-de ari-ma-sen	No, that is not a good book.

Sore-wa warui-hon-de su.	That is a bad book.
Anata-no hon-wa warui hon-de su ka?	Is your book a bad book?
Iie, watakushi-no hon-wa warui hon-de ari-masen.	No, my book is not a bad book.
Kore-wa donna hako-de su ka?	What kind of a box is this?
Sore-wa ookii hako-de su.	That is a big box.
Kore-wa donna hako-no futa-de su ka?	What kind of a box does this lid belong to?
ore-wa chiisai hako-no futa-de su	That lid belongs to a small box.
Kore-wa nan'-de su ka?	What is this?
Sore-wa watakushi-no ookii hankachi-de su.	That is my big handkerchief.
Kore-wa Kiyooka-san-no chiisai hon-de su.	This is Mr. Kiyooka's little book.
Anata-no-wa yoi hon-de su ka?	Is yours a good book?
Soo-de ari-masen, watakushi-no-wa yoi hon-de ari-masen	No, mine is not a good book.
Anata-no-wa donna teeburu-de su ka?	What kind of a table is yours?
Watakushi-no-wa ookii teeburu-de su.	Mine is a big table.

LESSON 6

Adjectives(2): Noun-Adjectives

Example:

Kore-wa kirei-na hon-de su. *This is a pretty book.*

this	pretty	book	is	*(and plural)*

Let us regard **-na** as a variation of **-no,** the possessive ending for nouns. Then, **kirei-na hon** literally means *book of beauty* or *book of prettiness.* The use of noun-adjectives is quite the same as that of the possessive case of nouns. In most cases the noun-adjectives are derivations from Chinese or other words of foreign origin while the regular adjectives are of pure Japanese origin and they have inflexions.

An English word, too, may be used as a noun-adjective, thus: **Anata-wa** *regular*-**na** *member*-**de su.** (*You are a regular member.*) This usage is sometimes used when the speaker finds that an English word is more expressive than a Japanese equivalent.

Key Word:

    -na   (*of*)

Vocabulary:

kirei-na	*pretty, clean*
kitanai (a regular adjective)	*ugly, dirty*
taisetsu-na	*precious, important*
taira-na	*flat, smooth*

" hoteru "   *hotel*

" shatsu "   *shirt,* especially *undershirt*

Exercises:

Kore-wa donna hon-de su ka?	What kind of a book is this?
Sore-wa kirei-na hon-de su	That is a pretty book.
Kore-wa nan'-de su ka?	What is this?
Sore-wa watakushi-no taise-tsu-na hon-de su.	That is my precious book.
Kore-wa taira-na hako-de su.	This is a flat box.
Kore-wa taira-na hako-no fu-ta-de su.	This is the lid for a flat box.
Kore-wa watakushi-no kita-nai shatsu-de su.	This is my dirty under-shirt.
Kore-wa watakushi-no kirei-na shatsu to kimono-de su	This is my clean under-shirt and kimono.
Kore-wa donna hoteru-de su ka?	What kind of a hotel is this?
Sore-wa ookii kirei-na hoteru-de su.	That is a big, beautiful hotel.
Anata-no-wa donna hako-de su ka?	What kind of a box is yours?
Watakushi-no-wa taira-na ki-rei-na hako-de su.	Mine is a flat, pretty box.
Sore-wa watakushi-no taise-tsu-na pen to inku-de su.	That is my precious pen and ink.
Kore-wa anata-no taisetsu-na shatsu-de su ka?	Is this your precious un-dershirt?

Sore-wa taisetsu-na shatsu-de ari-masen.	That is not a precious undershirt.
Anata-no-wa taira-na hako-de ari-masen ka ?	Isn't yours a flat box ?
Iie, watakushi-no-wa taira-na hako-de ari-masen.	No, mine is not a flat box

---

LESSON 7

Adjectives as Predicate: " This is good "

Examples

Kore-wa yoku ari-masu. (regular adjectives)

this	good	is	*This is good.*

Kore-wa kirei-de su. (noun-adjectives)

this	pretty	is	*This is pretty*

Compare the last syllable of the regular adjective **yoku** in the above example and that of **yoi** of the Lesson 5. When an adjective is used as predicate, it ends in **ku** and when it is used before a noun, it ends in **i**. This change in the end syllable is what we call the inflexion. In colloquial Japanese the inflexion of adjectives is " **i, ku, kere,**" and there is no irregular inflexion. The last ending, **kere,** will be taken up later in Lesson 51

The regular-adjectives are called in the form with the i-ending, as " the adjective **yoi.**"

The noun-adjectives, being nouns, are treated as such when they are used as predicate. Compare the following two sentences.

Kore-wa hon-de su.	*This is a book.*
Kore-wa kirei-de su.	*This is pretty.* (*This is a beauty.*)

The negative forms, as they may be expected, are as follows:

Kore-wa yoku ari-masen.	*This is not good.*
Kore-wa kirei-de ari-masen.	*This is not pretty.*

Key Words:

> —wa
> —ku ari-masu
> —ku ari-masen
> -de su
> -de ari-masen

Vocabulary:

hiroi	*wide, large in area*
semai	*narrow, small in area*
rippa-na	*magnificent, fine*
heya	*room*

Inflexion of Adjectives:

yoi	yoku	yokere
warui	waruku	warukere
ookii	ookiku	ookikere
chiisai	chiisaku	chiisakere
kitanai	kitanaku	kitanakere

hiroi	hiroku	hirokere
semai	semaku	semakere
taisetsu-na	taisetsu-de	
taira-na	taira-de	
rippa-na	rippa-de	

Exercises :

Kore-wa hiroi heya-de su ka ?	Is this a large room ?
Kore-wa hiroku ari-masu ka?	Is this wide ?
Soo-de su, kore-wa hiroi heya-de su.	Yes, this is a large room.
Soo-de su, kore-wa hiroku ari-masu.	Yes, this is wide.
Iie, kore-wa hiroi heya-de ari-masen.	No, this is not a large room.
Iie, kore-wa hiroku ari-masen.	No, this is not wide.
Sore-wa rippa-na heya-de su ka ?	Is that a fine room ?
Anata-no heya-wa rippa-de su ka ?	s your room fine ?
Watakushi-no heya-wa rippa-de su	My room is fine.
Watakushi-no-wa rippa-na heya-de su.	Mine is a fine room.
Watakushi-no heya-wa rippa-de ari-masen.	My room is not fine.
Watakushi-no-wa semai semai heya-de su.	Mine is a narrow, narrow (very narrow) room.
Hoteru-no heya-wa ookii heya-de su ka ?	re the rooms of the hotel big rooms ?

Iie, hoteru-no-wa kitanai semai heya-de su.

No, those of the hotel
are miserable, narrow
rooms.

LESSON 8

-WA and -GA

Examples :

Kore-wa watakushi-no-de su.   *This is mine.*
  this   mine   is

Kore-ga watakushi-no-de su.   *This is mine. (This*
  this   mine   is   *particular one is*
  mine.)

There are two endings for subject, **-wa** and **-ga,** of which
-wa is ordinarily used.   **-Ga** is used when the speaker
wishes to put particular emphasis on the subject, as
" This is mine and not that," or when he points out a particular one out of many.   Note the following sentences :

Kore-wa anata-no-de su ka ?
                Is this yours ?

Hai, kore-wa watakushi-no-de su.
                Yes, this is mine.

Kore-ga anata-no-de su ka ?
                Is this one yours ?

Note : In Lesson 7 strictly grammatical expressions are
given, but in actual speech a corrupted form, such as " Kore-wa
yoi-de su," is currently used. However, a student should begin
with the strictly correct form.

Hai, kore-ga watakushi-no-de su.
Yes, this one is mine.

Dore-ga anata-no-de su ka?
Which is yours?

Kore-ga watakushi-no-de su.
This one is mine.

In negative expressions **-wa** is generally used, because there is usually no emphasis on the subject.

Kore-wa anata-no-de ari-masen ka?
Isn't this yours?

Iie, kore-wa watakushi-no-de ari-masen.
No, this is not mine.

Kore-ga anata-no-de su ka?
Is this one yours?

Iie, kore-wa watakushi-no-de ari-masen.
No, this is not mine.

The distinction between **-wa** and **-ga** is one of the subtleties of the Japanese language. Their correct usage is a measure of skill in the language, but it is not absolutely essential in the communication of ideas. Therefore, if it is difficult, do not let it trouble you. Simply remember that **-ga** is a variation of **-wa** and because of its stronger tone, gives particular emphasis to the subject to which it is attached.

Key Words:

-wa	ending for subject in ordinary statement
-ga	emphatic ending for subject

Vocabulary :

dore (pronoun)	*which ? which one ?*
kono (adjective)	*this*
sono (adjective)	*that*
enpitsu	*pencil*

Attention is called to the distinction between **kono,** **sono** and **kore, sore,** because they are represented by the same English words, *this* and *that.* **Kono** and **sono** are always used with a noun, as **kono hon** or **sono hon** (*this book* or *that book*), but **kore** and **sore** are pronouns, always used independently, as **Kore-wa hon-de su** (*This is a book*).

Exercises :

Dore-ga anata-no enpitsu-de su ka ?	Which is your pencil ?
Kore-ga anata-no enpitsu-de su ka ?	Is this one your pencil ?
Soo-de su, kore-ga watakushi-no-de su.	Yes, this one is mine.
Iie, kore-wa watakushi-no enpitsu-de ari-masen.	No, this is not my pencil.
Kono hon-wa taisetsu-de su ka ?	Is this book important ?
Kono hon-ga taisetsu-na hon-de su ka ?	Is this the important book ?
Soo-de su, kono hon-ga taisetsu-na hon-de su.	Yes, this book is the important book.

Dore-ga anata-no taisetsu-na hon-de su ka ?	Which is your precious book ?
Kono hon-ga sore-de su.	This book is it.
Dore-ga Smith-san-de su ka ?	Which is Mr. Smith ?
Kono otoko-ga Smith-de su.	This man is Smith.
Anata-wa Smith-san-de su ka ?	Are you Mr. Smith ? (Is your name Smith ?)
Hai, watakushi-wa Smith-de su.	Yes, I am Mr. Smith. (My name is Smith.)
Anata-ga Smith-san-de su ka ?	Are you Mr. Smith ?
Hai, watakushi-ga Smith-de su.	Yes, I (and no one else) am Smith.
Soo-de ari-masen, watakushi-wa Smith-de ari-masen. Ko-re-ga Smith-san-de su.	No, I am not Mr. Smith. This is Mr. Smith.

LESSON 9

Sentences of the Type "Here is a book."

This is a book and its variations have been studied for the last eight lessons. Let us now take up another type of expressions which point out the position of things.

Examples :

| **Koko-ni hon-ga ari-masu.** | *Here is a book.* |
| here   book   is | *Here are some books.* |

Hon-wa koko-ni ari-masu.   *The book is here.*[1]

Substituting **heya** (*room*) for **koko,** one may say

Hon-wa heya-ni ari-masu.   *The book is in the room.*

Also, one may say

   Hon-ga ari-masu.   *There is a book.*

The word *there* has no significant meaning. Therefore it is natural that a corresponding word is lacking in the Japanese.

Key Words:

-wa	ending for subject
-ga	ending for subject
-ni	*in, on, at, to*
ari-masu	*is, are*

Vocabulary:

koko	*here*
soko	*there*
doko	*where?*
tana	*shelf*
heya	*room*

Note that the syllable of **do** usually denotes a question, as it is seen in **doko** (*where*), **dore** (*which*), **donna** (*what kind of*), **donata** (*who*). Also, the syllable of **ko** and **so** denote something near and something far, as **koko** (*here*) **kore** (*this*), **kono** (*this*) and **soko** (*there*), **sore** (*that*), **sono** (*that*).

Exercises:

   Koko-ni nani-ga ari-masu ka?   What is here?

---

[1] *-Wa* is used when an idea of "in the case of" or "if it is about—" is implied. Therefore, *Hon-wa koko-ni ari-masu* implies "If it is about the book you want to know, it is here."

Soko-ni hon to hako-ga ari-masu.	There are a book and a box there.
Kono heya-ni nani to nani-ga ari-masu ka?	What and what are in this room?
Kono heya-ni teeburu to tana-ga ari-masu.	In this room there are a table and a shelf.
Tana-ni nani-ga ari-masu ka?	What is on the shelf?
Pen to inku-ga ari-masu.	There are a pen and ink.
Hon-wa doko-ni ari-masu ka?	Where is the book?
Hon-wa tana-ni ari-masu.	The book is on the shelf.
Watakushi-no hon-wa doko-ni ari-masu ka?	Where is my book?
Anata-no kirei-na hon-wa hako-ni ari-masu.	Your pretty book is in the box.
Tana-ni donna hako-ga ari-masu ka?	What kind of a box is there on the shelf?
Tana-ni ookii hako-ga ari-masu.	There is a big box on the shelf.

LESSON 10

Here is a man.

Examples:

Koko-ni hito-ga i-masu

here   man   is

{ *Here is a man.*
{ *Here are several men.*

Hito-ga i-masu.　　　　{ *There is a man.*
　|　　　|　　　　　　　　{ *There are several men.*
　man　　is

Sono hito-wa heya-ni i-masu.

　　　　　　　　That man (he) is in the room.

The Japanese language makes distinction between living things and inanimate things.   For men, animals and general living things **i-masu** is used while for things which do not move—including trees and plants—**ari-masu** is used. This distinction applies in sentences of the above type only.   In *This is a book* and *This is a man*, **ari-masu** is invariably used, as **Kore-wa hon-de ari-ma-su (hon-de su)** and **Kore-wa hito-de ari-masu (hito-de su)**.

Key Words :

-wa, -ga	endings for subject
-ni	*in, on, at, to*
i-masu	*is, are, am*
i-masen	*is not, are not, am not*

Vocabulary :

hito	*person, man, woman*
sono hito	*he, she, that person*
inu	*dog*
mushi	*insect, worm*
ki	*tree*
niwa	*garden, yard*

The proper Japanese ward for *he* is **kare**, but it is not generally used in daily speech as being too literary.

Sono hito (*that person*) is used instead for both *he* and *she*.

Exercises:

Koko-ni donata-ga i-masu ka?	Who is here?
Koko-ni Smith-san-ga i-masu	Here is Mr. Smith.
Soko-ni nani-ga i-masu ka?	What is there?
Soko-ni inu-ga i-masu.	A dog is there.
Inu-wa doko-ni i-masu-ka?	Where is the dog?
Inu-wa niwa-ni i-masu.	The dog is in the yard.
Ki-wa doko-ni ari-masu ka?	Where is the tree?
Ki-wa niwa-ni ari-masu.	The tree is in the garden.
Niwa-ni donata-ga i-masu ka?	Who is in the garden?
Niwa-ni Kiyooka-san-ga i-masu.	There is Mr. Kiyooka in the garden.
Satoo-san-wa Tōkyō-ni i-masu ka?	Is Mr. Satoo in Tokyo? (Does Mr. Satoo live in Tokyo?)
Iie, Satoo-san-wa Tōkyō-ni i-masen.	No, Mr. Satoo is not in Tokyo. (Mr. Satoo does not live in Tokyo.)
Sono hito-wa Yokohama-ni i-masu ka?	Is he in Yokohama?
Soo-de su.	He is.

LESSON 11

In, On, Under

Examples:

Tana-no ue-ni hon-ga ari-masu.
| | | | |
shelf   on   book   is

> *There is a book on the shelf.* (and plural

Hon-wa tana-no ue-ni ari-masu.
| | | |
book   shelf   on   is

> *The book is on the shelf.* (and plural)

Key Words:

-wa, -ga	endings for subject
-no ue-ni	*on, upon*
ari-masu	*is, are* (for inanimate things)
i-masu	*is, are, am* (for living things)

-No ue-ni is exactly the English *on top of* arranged backwards.

-no   ue   -ni
| | |
of   top   on

The same is true with **-no naka-ni** and **-no shita-ni**. As **-ni** alone may stand for *in* or *on*, it depends upo the speaker's wish for preciseness to say either **Tana-ni hon-ga ari-masu** or **Tana-no ue-ni hon-ga ari-masu**.

Vocabulary:

-no naka-ni	*in, inside*

-no shita-ni	*under*
todana	*closet, cupboard*
honbako	*bookcase*
yuka	*floor*

Todana has been changed for euphonic reasons from **to-tana** (*door-shelf*) or *doored shelves*. The same is true with **honbako** which comes from **hon-hako**, *book-box*.

Exercises:

Anata-wa doko-ni i-masu ka?	Where are you?
Watakushi-wa heya-no naka-ni i-masu.	I am in the room.
Hon-wa doko-ni ari-masu ka?	Where is the book?
Hon-wa honbako-no naka-ni ari-masu.	The book is in the bookcase.
Ki-no shita-ni nani-ga i-masu ka?	What is under the tree?
Ki-no shita-ni inu-ga i-masu	Under the tree there is a dog.
Yuka-no ue-ni nani-ga ari-masu ka?	What is on the floor?
Yuka-no ue-ni todana to honbako-ga ari-masu.	On the floor there are a cupboard and a bookcase.
Inu-wa niwa-ni i-masu ka?	Is the dog in the yard?
Iie, inu-wa niwa-ni i-masen. Inu-wa heya-no naka-ni i-masu	No, the dog is not in the yard. The dog is in the room.
Sono hon-wa honbako-ni ari-masu ka?	Is that book in the bookcase?

Iie, sono hon-wa honbako-no naka-ni ari-masen. Sore-wa tana-no ue-ni ari-masu.

No, that book is not in the bookcase. It is on the shelf.

Sono hito-wa niwa-ni i-masu ka?

Is he in the garden?

Iie, sono hito-wa niwa-ni i-masen. Sono hito-wa anata-no heya-ni i-masu.

No, he is not in the garden. He is in your room.

LESSON 12

Behind, In Front Of, Etc.

Example:

Hako-no mae-ni hon-ga ari-masu.
> *There is a book in front of the box.*

This is continuation of the last lesson. There is little to explain.

Key Words:

-wa, -ga	endings for subject
-no mae-ni	*in front of*
ari-masu	*is, are*
i-masu	*is, are, am*

Mae, ushiro, ue, shita and all the words of the kind are nouns, and they can be used as such. Note the following sentences.

Kore-ga mae-de su.
> *This is the front.*

Kore-ga hako-no mae-de su.
> *This is the front of the box.*

Hako-wa migi-ni ari-masu.
> *The box is on the right.*

Vocabulary:

-no mae-ni	*in front of*
-no ushiro-ni	*behind*
-no migi-ni	*at the right side of*
-no hidari-ni	*at the left side of*
-no soba-ni	*at the side of, near*

Exercices:

Anata-wa doko-ni i-masu ka?	Where are you?
Watakushi-wa ki-no soba-ni i-masu.	I am by the tree.
Teeburu-no ushiro-ni nani-ga ari-masu ka?	What is behind the table?
Teeburu-no ushiro-ni todana-ga ari-masu.	Behind the table is a cupboard.
Anata-no migi-ni nani-ga ari-masu ka?	What is on your right?
Watakushi-no migi-ni hon-ba-ko-ga ari-masu.	There is a bookcase on my right.
Inu-wa anata-no soba-ni i-masu ka?	Is the dog at your side?
Iie, inu-wa koko-ni i-masen.	No, the dog is not here.
Teeburu-no ue-ni naifu to fo-oku-ga ari-masu.	There are knives and forks on the table.

Naifu-wa migi-ni ari-masu Fooku-wa hidari-ni ari-masu. Chiisai naifu-wa mae-ni ari-masu	The knife is on the right. The fork is on the left. The small knife is at the front.
Kore-wa honbako-no mae-de su. Kore-ga ushiro-de su.	This is the front of the bookcase. This is the back.
Mae-wa kirei-de su. Ushiro-wa kirei-de ari-masen.	The front is pretty. The back is not pretty.
Kore-ga watakushi-no migi-de su	This is my right.
Kore-ga watakushi-no hidari-de su.	This is my left.
Kore-ga kono hako-no ue to shita-de su.	This is the top of the box and the bottom.
Kono hako-no naka-wa kirei-de su.	The inside of this box is clean.

LESSON 13

Negation of Adjectives : "Unimportant"

Example :

Kore-wa taisetsu-de-nai hon-de su.

this   unimportant   book   is

This is an unimportant book.

Much like in English there are two ways to express the negation of adjectives. The above example shows one of the ways, and the other is by the use of negation with the verb as it was studied in Lessons 5 and 6 :—

Kore-wa taisetsu-na hon-de ari-masen.
> *This is not an important book.*

The use of *un* in English is limited to a few adjectives, but in Japanese **-de-nai** can be applied to any noun-adjectives.

Nai is an adjective and it has an inflexion of a regular adjective.

taisetsu-de-nai taisetsu-de-naku taisetsu-de-nakere
  unimportant
kirei-de-nai kirei-de-naku kirei-de-nakere
  not pretty
taira-de-nai taira-de-naku taira-de-nakere
  not flat

etc.

The regular adjectives also can be turned negative in very much the same way :

Examples :

Kore-wa ookiku-nai hako-de su.
  this   big   not   box   is
> *This is not a big box.*

Kore-wa ookii hako-de ari-masen.
> *This is not a big box.*

The inflexion of **nai** when used with regular adjectives is as follows — it is much like that when used with the noun-adjectives :

ookiku-nai	ookiku-naku	ookiku-nakere
not big		
chiisaku-nai	chiisaku-naku	chiisaku-nakere
not small		
yoku-nai	yoku-naku	yoku-nakere
not good		
waruku-nai	waruku-naku	waruku-nakere
not bad		
takaku-nai	takaku-naku	takaku-nakere
not high		

etc.

The distinction between the two ways of negation is rather subtle, but it is much like in English as one may sense the difference between " This is not important" and " This is unimportant." In interrogative form the distinction is clearer. " **Kore-wa ookiku-nai hako-de su ka ?** " means simply " Is this a small box ?" But " **Kore-wa ookii hako-de ari-masen ka ?** " means " Isn't this a big box ?" implying something more than a simple question. However, this kind of subtleties are beyond our scope for the moment.

Key Words :

> -nai, -naku   *not, un—, in—*
>   (used after regular adjectives)
>
> -de-nai, -de-naku   *not, un, in—*
>   (used after noun-adjectives)

Vocabulary:

shinsetsu-na	*kind*
rikoo-na	*wise, intelligent*
takai	*high, expensive*
mono	*thing*

Exercises:

Sore-wa shinsetsu-na hito-de su ka?	Is that a kind man?
Sore-wa shinsetsu-na hito-de ari-masen.	That is not a kind man.
Sore-wa shinsetsu-de-nai hito de su.	That is an unkind man.
Mushi-wa rikoo-na mono-de su ka?	Is an insect an intelligent thing?
Mushi-wa rikoo-de-nai mono-de su.	An insect is not an intelligent thing.
Koko-ni takai hon-ga ari-ma-su.	Here is an expensive book.
Koko-ni takaku-nai hon-ga ari-masu.	Here is an inexpensive book.
Takaku-nai mono-wa doko-ni ari-masu ka?	Where are the inexpensive things?
Takaku-nai mono-wa koko-ni ari-masu.	Inexpensive things are here.
Koko-ni takaku-nai mono-wa ari-masen.	There is no inexpensive thing here.

LESSON 14

Compound Sentences with BUT and AND

Examples:

Kono inu-wa kirei-de su, soshite sono inu-wa rikoo-de su.

> *This dog is pretty, and that dog is clever.*

Kono inu-wa kirei-de su, soshite rikoo-de su.

> *This dog is pretty, and (he) is clever.*

Compound sentences are nothing more than two or more
simple sentences connected together with **soshite** (*and*)
or **keredomo** (*but*). However, when the same subject is
repeated in the second clause, it is usually understood.
Of course, the subject may be repeated if the speaker
wishes to place special emphasis on it, as:

Kono inu-wa kirei-de su, soshite kono inu-wa rikoo-de su.

> *This dog is pretty, and also this dog is clever.*

Key Words:

soshite	*and, also*
keredomo	*but*

Soshite is used in connecting clauses only; for connecting words **to** is used, as **pen to inku** (*pen and ink*). See
Lesson 4.

Vocabulary:

uchi	*house, home*

gakkoo	*school*
taihen	*very, unusually*
" desuku "	*desk*

Exercises :

Kore-wa kirei-na inu-de su, keredomo rikoo-de ari-ma-sen.

This is a pretty dog, but he is not clever.

Kore-wa ookii uchi-de su, soshite taihen kirei-de su.

This is a big house, and it is very pretty.

Kono uchi-wa ookiku ari-ma-sen, keredomo taihen yoi uchi-de su.

This house is not big, but it is a very good house.

Koko-ni watakushi-no desuku-ga ari-masu, soshite soko-ni anata-no-ga ari-masu.

Here is my desk, and there is yours.

Anata-no gakkoo-wa donna gakkoo-de su ka ?

What kind of a school is your school ?

Watakushi-no gakkoo-wa tai-hen chiisai gakkoo-de su, keredomo taihen rippa-de su.

My school is a very small school, but it is very fine.

Anata-no desuku-wa doko-ni ari-masu ka ?

Where is your desk ?

Watakushi-no desuku-wa ko-ko-ni ari-masen, keredomo uchi-ni ari-masu.

My desk is not here, but it is at home (in my house).

Kimono to shatsu-wa doko-ni ari-masu ka ?

Where are the dress and the shirt ?

Kimono-wa todana-ni ari-ma-su, soshite shatsu-wa tana-no ue-ni ari-masu.

The dress is in the closet and the shirt is on the shelf.

Hon to pen to inku-wa doko-ni ari-masu ka?	Where are the book and the pen and the ink?
Hon-wa honbako-ni ari-masu, soshite pen to inku-wa desu-ku no ue-ni ari-masu.	The book is in the book-case, and the pen and ink are on the desk.
Watakushi-no uchi to anata-no uchi-wa gakkoo-no mae-ni ari-masu, soshite Smith-san-no uchi-wa gakkoo-no ushiro-ni ari-masu.	My house and your house are in front of the school, and Smith's house is at the back of the school.

LESSON 15

Ari-masu and I-masu

Examples:

Koko-ni hito-ga i-masu.   *Here is a person.*

Kono hito-wa ookiku ari-masu.   *This person is big.*

The distinction between **ari-masu** and **i-masu** has been studied already (Lesson 10). The purpose of this lesson is to remind the students that in descriptive expressions **ari-masu** is used for both animate and inanimate things. It is convenient to remember that **i-masu** is used where the meaning of "to stay" is implied. For instance, *Here is a person* can imply that the person stays here of his own accord, and **i-masu** is used. In **Koko-ni hon-ga ari-masu** the book does not stay here—it is here, because it was placed here—and **ari-masu** is used. In **Kono hi-to-wa ookiku ari-masu** the subject is an animate thing but there is no implication of staying; it is a simple statement that the person is big, and **ari-masu** is used

Note the special use of **i-masu** in the following sentences:

Kono hito-wa kirei-de i-masu.
This person is still pretty. (*This person stays pretty.*)
Kono hito-wa kirei-de su (ari-masu).
This person is pretty

We shall study the use of **i-masu** further in the lessons on Progressive Form (Lesson 18).

Vocabulary:

Nippon	*Japan*
Nippon-no	*of Japan, Japanese*
mado	*window*
tatami	*reed mat*
tsukue	*table, desk*
hibachi	*fire brazier*
itsumo	*always*
shooji	*paper door*, with single layer of light paper

Exercises:

(See the illustration for Lesson 16)

Kore-wa rippa-na heya-de su.	This is a fine room.
Kore-wa rippa-na Nippon-no heya-de su.	This is a fine Japanese room.
Heya-no hidari-ni mado-ga ari-masu, soshite mado-no tana-ni hako-ga ari-masu.	There is a window to the left of the room, and on the shelf of the window there is a box.

Migi-ni tana-ga ari-masu, so-shite tana-no ue-ni chiisai todana-ga ari-masu.

To the right there is a shelf, and above the shelf there is a small closet.

Yuka-no ue-ni nani-ga ari-masu ka?

What is on the floor?

Nippon-no heya-no yuka-no ue-ni itsumo tatami-ga ari-masu.

Over the floor of a Japanese room there is tatami always.

Kirei-na tatami-wa yoi mono-de su.

Clean tatami is a good thing (to look at).

Kirei-de-nai tatami-wa yoku-nai mono-de su.

Unclean tatami is not a good thing (to look at).

Tatami-no ue-ni nani to nani-ga ari-masu ka?

What (and what) are on the floor?

Tsukue to hibachi-ga ari-masu.

There are a table and a fire brazier.

Kore-wa rippa-na ookii tsuku-e-de su, keredomo hibachi-wa rippa-de ari-masen.

This is a fine big table, but the fire brazier is not fine.

Hibachi-no soba-ni hito-ga i-masu.

There is a person (or persons) by the fire brazier.

Sono hito-wa kirei-de su ka?

Is that person (she) pretty?

Soo-de su, sono hito-wa itsu-mo kirei-de i-masu, soshite shinsetsu-de su.

Yes, she is always pretty, and kind.

Mado-ni shooji-ga ari-masu.

There are paper doors in the window.

Kore-wa chiisai shooji-de su.

These are small paper doors.

Shooji-wa hako-no ushiro-ni ari-masu.

The paper doors are behind the box.

LESSON 16

Review Lesson

Zashiki

Vocabulary:

zashiki	*parlour*
tokonoma	*alcove* (like the mantel-piece to-konoma gives beauty and formality to a room)
kakemono	*hanging scroll*
okimono	*an ornament* (**oki** = *to set,* **mono** = *thing*)
kabin	*flower vase*
o-kyaku	*guest* (**o-** is an honorific)
o-cha	*tea* (**o-** is an honorific)

tabako-bon	*tobacco tray*
tenjoo	*ceiling*
dentoo	*electric light*
kabe	*wall*
fusuma	*heavy paper door*
zabuton	*cushion*

Exercises :

Kono heya-wa Nippon-no za-shiki-de su.

This room is a Japanese parlour.

Kore-wa taihen rippa-na za-shiki-de su.

This is a very fine parlour.

Tokonoma-ni itsumo kirei-na mono-ga ari-masu.

In the alcove there is always something pretty.

Kono zashiki-no tokonoma-ni kakemono to okimono-ga ari-masu.

In the alcove of this parlour there are hanging scroll and an ornament.

Sono kakemono-wa taihen ki-rei-de su, soshite rippa-de su.

That hanging scroll is very pretty, and fine.

Okimono-wa taihen rippa-de su, keredomo ookiku ari-masen.

The ornament is very fine, but it is not large.

Hidari-ni taihen ookii rippa-na kabin-ga ari-masu.

On the left there is a very large and fine flower vase.

Tokonoma-no mae-ni hito-ga i-masu.

In front of the alcove there is a person.

Sono hito-wa o-kyaku-de su.

That person (she) is a guest.

O-kyaku-wa itsumo tokono-ma-no mae-ni i-masu.

A guest is always in front of the alcove.

Hidari-no hito-wa uchi-no hi-to-de su.

The person on the left is the person of the house (the host).

Uchi-no hito-wa tokonoma-no mae-ni i-masen.

The person of the house (the host) is not in front of the alcove.

Taisetsu-na hito-wa itsumo to-konoma-no mae-ni i-masu.

An important person is always in front of the alcove.

(The above sentences will be more natural if a word for "to sit" could be used in place of i-masu. But that is beyond our scope now.)

O-kyaku-no mae-ni o-cha-ga ari-masu.

There is a tea in front of the guest.

O-kyaku to uchi-no hito-no mae-ni o-cha-ga ari-masu.

In front of the guest and the host there are some teas.

O-cha to tabako-bon-wa tsu-kue-no ue-ni ari-masu.

The tea and the tobacco tray are on the table.

Kono heya-no mono-wa rip-pa-de su.

The things in this room are fine.

Kono zashiki-wa itsumo kirei-de su.

This parlour is always clean.

LESSON 17

Sentences of the type "I open a box."

Examples:

Watakushi-wa hako-wo ake-masu.

| | | |
| I | box | open |

I open a box.

Watakushi-wa hako-wo ake-masen.

I do not open a box.

Now that we have practically exhausted all the variations of the types of sentences "This is a book" and "There is a book," we are turning to another type which expresses actions.

Key Words:

-wa, -ga	endings for subject
-wo	ending for object
-masu	(*do*), an auxiliary verb

-Masu has been explained as an auxiliary verb which has a usage analogous to that of the English *do* (Lesson 3). However, **-masu** is used to give a certain respectfulness to the expression while *do* is usually employed in giving emphasis, as in "I do open a box." In Japanese there is a more blunt way of expressing the same idea without the use of **-masu** which will be taken up in Lesson 40.

Vocabulary:

ake   *open*

shime	*close*
shi	*do* (a verb)
yomi	*read*
shinbun	*newspaper*

Exercises:

Anata-wa nani-wo ake-masu ka?	What do you open?
Watakushi-wa hon-wo ake-masu.	I open a book.
Anata-wa nani-wo shi-masu ka?	What do you do?
Watakushi-wa hon-wo ake-masu, soshite sore-wo yomi-masu.	I open a book and read it.
Sono hito-wa shinbun-wo yomi-masu ka?	Does he read a newspaper?
Hai, sono hito-wa itsumo shinbun-wo yomi-masu.	Yes, he always reads newspaper.
Watakushi-no heya-ni hon-ga ari-masu, keredomo watakushi-wa sore-wo yomi-masen.	There are some books in my room, but I do not read them.
Anata-wa mado-wo shime-masu.	You close the window.
Watakushi-wa mado-no shooji-wo shime-masu.	I close the paper door of the window.
Kono hito-wa nani-wo shi-masu ka?	What does this man do?
Kono hito-wa hon-wo yomi-masu, keredomo shinbun-wo yomi-masen.	He reads books, but he does not read newspapers.

LESSON 18

Progressive Form: "I am opening a box."

Examples:

Watakushi-wa hako-wo ake-te-i-masu.
I   box   opening am
I am opening a box.

Watakushi-wa hako-wo ake-te-i-masen.
I am not opening a box.

It is interesting to see that both English and Japanese make use of the verb *to be* (**i-masu**) in forming the progressive. However, the fundamental idea is different. **Ake-te-i-masu** literally means *open and be,* or *open and stay opening,* the word **te** being a connective *and.* Therefore, in **ake-te-i-masu** there is no idea of the progression of action, rather it denotes staying in the same condition. In certain cases, such as with **mochi** (*to have*) the Japanese progressive form cannot be translated into English progressive form :—

Watakushi-wa hon-wo motte-i-masu.
I have a book.

Motte-i-masu is a contraction of **mochi-te-i-masu** which does not mean *I am having a book* or *I am in the process of acquiring a book,* but it means *I possess a book and I stay so.* A student should remember the difference, but in majority of cases the progressive form of one language can be turned right into that of the other.

Key Words:

-te-i-masu	*is, are, am —ing*
-te-i-masen	*is, are, am, not —ing*

Note that -te-i-masu is used for both animate and inanimate things.

Vocabulary:

mi		*see*
mochi	(motte-i-masu)	*have*
tachi	(tatte-i-masu)	*stand*
suwari	(suwatte-i-masu)	*sit*
yomi	(yonde-i-masu)	*read*

The last syllable of the verbs are often euphonically contracted when they are followed by **-te-i-masu**. The contracted forms are printed in the parenthesis.

Exercises:

Anata-wa mado-wo ake-te-i-masu ka?	Are you opening the window?
Hai, watakushi-wa mado-wo ake-te-i-masu.	Yes, I am opening the window.
Iie, watakushi-wa mado-wo ake-te-i-masen.	No, I am not opening the window.
Watakushi-wa sore-wo shime-te-i-masu.	I am closing it.
Anata-wa nani-wo shi-te-i-masu ka?	What are you doing?
Watakushi-wa shinbun-wo mi-te-i-masu.	I am looking at the news-paper.

Watakushi-wa hon-wo yonde-i-masu	I am reading a book.
Anata-wa soko-ni nani-wo mo-tte-i-masu ka?	What have you there?
Watakushi-wa koko-ni hon-wo motte-i-masu.	I have a book here.
Niwa-ni ookii ki-ga tatte-i-masu.	A big tree stands in the garden.
Ki-no shita-ni inu-ga tatte-i-masu.	A dog is standing under the tree.
Watakushi-wa inu-no soba-ni suwatte-i-masu.	I am sitting by the dog.
Watakushi-wa tachi-masu, so shite anata-wa suwari-masu.	I stand up and you sit down.
Watakushi-wa tatte-i-masu, soshite anata-wa suwatte-i-masu.	I am standing and you are sitting.

LESSON 19

Past Tense with -Masu

Examples:

Watakushi-wa hako-wo ake-mashita.

  | | |

 I   box   opened

I opened a box.

Watakushi-wa hako-wo ake-masen-deshita.

I did not open a box.

In the above examples the past tense and its negation

are indicated by the inflexion of **masu**. The verb **ake** has its own past tense and other forms which will have to be studied later (Lesson 40), but for the present we shall limit our scope to the above type which is respectful and safe for all persons to use. Also, it is very convenient as the knowledge of the inflexion of **masu** alone enables one to make use of all the Japanese verbs in simple expressions.

Just as **-de ari-masu** is contracted into **-de su,** its past form **-de ari-mashita** is contracted to **-de shita** (*was, were*) in daily speech. Its negative form is not contracted—**-de ari-masen-deshita** (*was not, were not*).

Key Words:

-mashita	suffix for past tense (*did*)
-masen-deshita	*did not*
-de shita (-de ari-mashita)	*was, were*
-de ari-masen-deshita	*was not, were not*

Vocabulary:

ki	*come*
-kara	*from, since*
kinoo	*yesterday*
itsu	*when?*

Exercises:

Anata-wa mado-wo ake-mashita ka?

Did you open the window?

Iie, watakushi-wa mado-wo ake-masen-deshita.

No, I did not open the window.

Anata-wa shinbun-wo yomi-mashita ka?	Did you read the newspaper?
Hai, watakushi-wa shinbun-wo yomi-mashita.	Yes, I read the newspaper.
Sore-wa yoi shinbun-de shita ka?	Was it a good newspaper?
Soo-de su, sore-wa yoi shinbun-de shita.	Yes, it was a good newspaper.
Iie, sore-wa yoi shinbun-de ari-masen-deshita.	No, it was not a good newspaper.
Sono hon-wa honbako-no naka-ni ari-mashita ka?	Was that book in the bookcase?
Sono hon-wa kinoo hon-bako-ni ari-mashita.	That book was in the bookcase yesterday.
Sono hon-wa kinoo honbako-ni ari-masen-deshita	That book was not in the bookcase yesterday.
Anata-wa kinoo Tōkyō-ni i-mashita ka?	Were you in Tokyo yesterday?
Hai, watakushi-wa Tōkyō-ni i-mashita.	Yes, I was in Tokyo.
Iie, watakushi-wa Tōkyō-ni i-masen-deshita.	No, I was not in Tokyo.
Anata-wa doko-kara ki-mashita ka?	Where did you come from?
Watakushi-wa Kamakura-kara ki-mashita.	came from Kamakura.
Anata-wa itsu ki-mashita ka?	When did you come?
Watakushi-wa kinoo ki-mashita.	I came yesterday.
Sono hito-wa itsu doko-kara ki-mashita ka?	When and from where did he come?

Sono hito-wa kinoo Yokoha-   He came from Yokoha-
ma-kara ki-mashita.   ma yesterday.

LESSON 20

Present Perfect: " I have been here since yesterday."

Example :

Watakushi-wa kinoo-kara koko-ni i-masu.

I	yesterday	since	here	have been

I have been here since yesterday.

The classic Japanese is most complete in its tense forms, but in the modern spoken Japanese all the elaborate, but annoying, forms have been eliminated even to the extent of perfect tenses such as *have been* and *had been.* Therefore, the English perfect tenses must be expressed either by a present tense or past tense in the Japanese. Strictly speaking, the above example means *I have been here since yesterday, and I continue to be here* If I am leaving or have left the place, the past tense must be used:—**Watakushi-wa kinoo-kara koko-ni i-mashita.**

The present perfect of other verbs than **ari-masu** and **i-masu**—e. g *I have been reading it* or *I have read it*—will be taken up in Lesson 25.

Vocabulary :

iki   *go*

ima	*now*
-made	*until, as far as*
gakkoo	*school*

-Made and **-kara** are used for both time and place. Also, **-ni** may be used for both time and place:

Watakushi-wa Tōkyō-ni iki-masu.
> *I go to Tokyo.*

Watakushi-wa Tōkyō-made iki-masu.
> *I go as far as Tokyo.*

Exercises:

Anata-wa itsu-kara koko-ni i-masu ka?	Since when have you been here?
Watakushi-wa kinoo-kara koko-ni i-masu.	I have been here since yesterday.
Anata-wa ima-made doko-ni i-mashita ka?	Where have you been until now?
Watakushi-wa ima-made uchi-ni i-mashita.	I have been home till just now.
Anata-wa itsu-made uchi-ni i-mashita ka?	Until when were you at home?
Watakushi-wa ima-made uchi-ni i-mashita.	Until just now I was in my house.
Anata-wa ima doko-ni iki-masu ka?	Where do you go now? (Where are you going now?)
Watakushi-wa ima gakkoo-ni iki-masu.	I go to school now.
Anata-wa doko-made iki-masu ka?	How far (as far as where) are you going?

Watakushi-wa gakkoo-made iki-masu.	I go as far as the school.
Anata-wa kinoo-kara doko-made yomi-mashita ka?	How far did you read since yesterday?
Watakushi-wa koko-made yo-mi-mashita.	I have read as far as here.
Sono hito-wa uchi-ni i-masu ka?	Is he at home?
Sono hito-wa kinoo-kara uchi-ni i-masen.	He has not been home since yesterday.

LESSON 21

" Let us open the box "

Examples:

Haku-wo ake-mashoo.   *Let us open the box.*

Haku-wo ake-mashoo ka?   *Shall we open the box?*

The subject is usually understood, because in this kind of expressions the subject is invariably " I " or " we," and there is no need of mentioning it. However, in special cases it may be mentioned:

Watakushi-ga ake-mashoo.
    Let ME open. (I will open it.)

Watakushi-ga ake-mashoo ka?
    Shall I open it? (Do you want me to open it?

" Let us not open the box " can not be expressed in

Japanese by the negation of **mashoo**. It has to be ex
pressed by saying, "Let us stop opening the box." This
will be studied when we take up complex sentences.

Key Word :

>   -mashoo   *will, shall, let us*

Vocabulary :

kai	*buy*
nori	*ride*
nomi	*drink*
mizu	*water*
densha	*street car* (**den** = *electric*, **sha** = *car*

Exercises :

Nani-wo ake-mashoo ka ?	What shall we open ?
Hako-wo ake-mashoo.	Let us open the box.
Nani-wo kai-mashoo ka ?	What shall we buy ?
Kirei-na kimono-wo kai-ma- shoo.	Let us buy a pretty dress.
Doko-ni iki-mashoo ka ?	Where shall we go ?
Anata-no uchi-ni iki-mashoo.	Let us go to your house.
Itsu anata-no uchi-ni iki-ma- shoo ka ?	When shall we go to your house ?
Ima iki-mashoo.	Let us go now.
Nani-wo nomi-mashoo ka ?	What shall we drink ?
Mizu-wo nomi-mashoo ka ?	Shall we drink some water ?
Hai, soo shi-mashoo.	Yes, let us do so.
Ima nani-wo shi-mashoo ka ?	What shall we do now ?

Densha-ni nori-mashoo, soshi-te uchi-ni iki-mashoo.	Let us ride in the street car, and let us go home.
Kono densha-wa doko-ni iki-masu ka?	Where does this street car go?
Kore-wa Yokohama-ni iki-masu.	This goes to Yokohama.
Kono densha-ni nori-mashoo ka?	Shall we take (ride in this street car?
Soo shi-mashoo.	Let us do so.

LESSON 22

Future

Examples:

Sono hito-ga hako-wo ake-mashoo.
He will open the box.

Sono hito-wa hako-wo ake-masen-deshoo.
He will not open the box.

Kore-wa yoi hon-de shoo (-de ari-mashoo).
This probably is a good book.

Kore-wa yoi hon-de ari-masen-deshoo.
This probably is not a good book.

-De shoo is an abbreviation of -de-ari-mashoo.

Key Words:

| -mashoo | *will, shall* |
| -masen-deshoo | *will not, shall not* |

| -de shoo (-de ari-mashoo) | *will be, shall be* |
| -de ari-masen-deshoo | *will not be, shall not be* |

The use of future form in Japanese is rather subtle and it makes one realize that a language is after all an expression of free thinking mind and that one language cannot always be translated into another by mechanical substitution of the words.   Strictly speaking the spoken Japanese has no tense to correspond with the future these of the European languages.

Mashoo is a form of the auxiliary verb **masu** which indicates uncertainty or desire.   And because uncertainty and desire are usually concerned with the future occurrences, this **mashoo** is generally called the future form of **masu**   **Mashoo** expresses the idea more akin to the subjunctive mood than future tense.

Therefore, when speaking of opening a box, a student should not concern himself too much with the time of opening.   Rather, he should think and feel, as the Japanese do, whether it should be expressed as a fixed action or uncertain action or an action to be desired. If it is fixed and certain, use present tense:

Sono hito-ga ashita sono hako-wo ake-masu.
   He opens the box tomorrow.

If there is some uncertainty or his willingness about opening it:

Sono hito-ga sono hako-wo ake-mashoo.
   He will open the box.

If the desire to open is the chief thought:

Kono hako-wo ima ake-mashoo.
> *Let us open the box now.*

Kono hako-wo ashita ake-mashoo.
> *Let us open the box tomorrow.*

The Japanese people feel that a show of uncertainty in speech is more respectful than a blunt, direct expression. Therefore, **mashoo** and **de shoo** are often used for such purpose:

Kore-wa yoi hon-de su ka?
> *Is this a good book?* (a direct question)

Kore-wa yoi hon-de shoo ka?
> *Is this a good book?* (a respectful inquiry)

Kore-wa yoi hon-de su.
> *This is a good book.* (an uncompromising answer)

Kore-wa yoi hon-de shoo.
> *This is a good book.* (a modest answer)

Not only **mashoo** but many other usages of the spoken Japanese will appear strange to one who is trained in formal grammar. But if he examines closely the spoken English—especially the informal slangish English—he will find that English, too, is discarding the rule of old grammar and is somewhat approaching the free usages of the spoken Japanese.

Vocabulary:

gohan   *boiled rice*, also *a repast*

" jamu "	*jam*
" pan " (from Spanish)	*bread*
" bata "	*butter*
" sandowitchi "	*sandwich*
ashita	*tomorrow*

Exercises :

Sono hito-wa itsu ki-mashoo ka ?	When will he come ?
Sono hito-wa itsu ki-masu ka ?	When does he come ?
Sono hito-wa ashita ki-ma-shoo.	He will come tomorrow.
Sono hito-wa ashita ki-masu.	He comes tomorrow.
Kono hito-wa pan to bata-wo tabe-mashoo ka ?	Will he eat bread and butter ?
Hai, kono hito-wa pan to bata-wo tabe-mashoo.	Yes, he will eat bread and butter.
Kono hito-wa pan-wo tabe-ma-su, keredomo gohan-wo ta-be-masen-de shoo.	He eats bread, but he probably will not eat rice.
Kore-wa bata-no sandowitchi-de shoo ka ?	Is this butter-sandwich ?
Iie, soo-de ari-masen-deshoo	No, it is not.
Kore-wa nan'-de shoo ka ?	What is this ?
Sore-wa jamu-no sandowitchi--de su.	This is a jam-sandwich.
Kore-wa yoi pan-de shoo ka ?	Is this a good bread ?
Hai, sore-wa taihen yoi pan-de su.	Yes, that is a very good bread.
Sore-wa yoi pan-de ari-masen-de shoo.	That is not a good bread.

Sono hito-wa ashita Yokoha-ma-ni iki-mashoo ka?	Will he go to Yokohama tomorrow?
Iie, sono hito-wa iki-masen-de-shoo.	No, he will not go.

LESSON 23

Progressive Form in Past and Future

Examples :

Watakushi-wa hako-wo ake-te-i-mashita.
I was opening the box.

Watakushi-wa hako-wo ake-te-i-masen-deshita.
I was not opening the box.

Watakushi-wa hako-wo ake-te-i-mashoo.
I will be opening the box.

Watakushi-wa hako-wo ake-te-i-masen-deshoo.
I will not be opening the box.

Key Words :

-te-i-mashita	*was, were —ing*
-te-i-masen-deshita	*was, were not—ing*
-te-i-mashoo	*will, shall be —ing*
-te-i-masen-deshoo	*will, shall not be —ing*

The Japanese progressive forms are very long and they may appear cumbersome to a new student. But they must be learned thoroughly and pronounced as if the whole strings of words were mere endings of the verb.

Vocabulary :

tori (totte-i-)	*take, catch*
kaki (kaite-i-)	*write*
tegami	*letter*
niku	*meat*

Exercises :

Anata-wa nani-wo shi-te-i-ma-shita ka ?	What were you doing ?
Watakushi-wa hon-wo yonde-i-mashita	I was reading a book.
Watakushi-wa hako-no futa-wo totte-i-mashita.	I was taking (off) the lid of a box.
Anata-wa ima mushi-wo totte-i-mashita ka ?	Were you catching the insects just now ?
Hai, watakushi-wa ki-no mu-shi-wo totte-i-mashita.	Yes, I was catching the insects of a tree.
Iie, watakushi-wa mushi-wo totte-i-masen-deshita.	No, I was not catching the insects.
Anata-wa nani-wo kaite-i-ma-shita ka ?	What were you writing ?
Watakushi-wa tegami-wo ka-ite-i-mashita.	I was writing a letter.
Anata-wa pan to niku-wo ta-be-te-i-mashita ka ?	Were you eating the bread and meat ?
Watakushi-wa pan-wo ta-be-te-i-masen-deshita, gohan to niku-wo tabe-te-i-mashita.	I was not eating the bread, I was eating the rice and the meat.
Sono hito-wa ashita nani-wo shi-te-i-mashoo ka ?	What will he be doing tomorrow ?

Sono hito-wa uchi-ni tegami-wo kaite-i-mashoo.

He will be writing a letter home.

Sono hito-wa tegami-wo kaite-i-masen-deshoo.

He will not be writting a letter.

LESSON 24

Verbs in Succession

Example:

Watakushi-wa sore-wo shi-te-mi-mashoo.

I	it	do and see	will

I will do it and see (I will try it).

The use of verbs in succession is one of the convenient peculiarities of the Japanese language. Here are some more examples:

ake-te-mi-masu	*open and see—examine the inside*
ake-te-iki-masu	*open and go—leave (something) open*
motte-ki-masu	*hold and come—bring*
motte-iki-masu	*hold and go—take away*
itte-ki-masu	*go and come—take a round trip, have been to*
shi-te-mi-masu	*do and see—try*
mi-te-mi-masu	*look and see—examine*
shi-te-iki-masu	*do and go—do before going*
shi-te-i-masu	*do and be—be doing (progressive form)*

The above list shows some of the more common examples, but any verbs may be put together according to necessity or speaker's desire. Sometimes three or four or five verbs may be strung along, such being the flexibility of the Japanese language. No doubt, there are briefer and more formal words to express the same ideas, but the above combinations are preferred in daily speech.

As seen in the last of the above examples, the progressive form is one of the common examples of the verbs in succession. Also, a succession of verbs may be made progressive, as:

Watakushi-wa sore-wo shi-te-mi-te-i-masu.
I am trying it.

Because the combination of verbs is to be taken a a unit, some care is necessary in translating their negative forms:

Watakushi-wa sore-wo shi-te-mi-masen-deshita.
I did not try it (I did not do it nor see about it).

Watakushi-wa sore-wo motte-ki-masen-deshita.
I did not bring it (I did not bring it, but I came.)
In the first example the negation applies to both verbs but in the second example the negation applies to the first verb (**mochi**) only.

Vocabulary:

aruki	*walk*
aruite-iki- (**aruki-te-iki-**)	*go on foot*
de	*go out, come out*

de-te-iki-

go out

de-te-ki-

come out

Exercises:

Kono hako-wo ake-te-mi-ma-shoo ka?

Shall we open this box and see?

Hai, ake-te-mi-mashoo.

Yes, let us open it and see.

Anata-wa hon-wo motte-ki-mashita ka?

Did you bring the book?

Iie, watakushi-wa hon-wo mo-tte-ki-masen-deshita.

No, I did not bring the book.

Kinoo anata-wa doko-ni itte-ki-mashita ka?

Where did you go yester-day.

Watakushi-wa kinoo Yokoha-ma-ni itte-ki-mashita.

I made a trip to Yoko-hama yesterday.

Anata-wa gakkoo-ni nani-wo motte-iki-masu ka?

What do you take to school?

Watakushi-wa hon-wo motte-iki-masu.

I take some books with me.

Inu-wa heya-kara de-te-ki-ma-shita ka?

Did the dog come out of the room?

Hai, inu-wa de-te-ki-mashita, soshite niwa-ni de-te-iki-ma-shita.

Yes, the dog came out, and he went out to the yard.

Anata-wa aruite-ki-mashita-ka?

Did you come on foot?

Soo-de su, watakushi-wa arui-te-ki-mashita.

Yes, I came on foot.

Gakkoo-ni aruite-iki-mashoo.

Let us walk to the school.

Kono todana-wo mi-te-mi-ma-shoo ka?	Shall we examine this closet?
Hai, mi-te-mi-mashoo.	Yes, let us examine it.
Sono hito-wa sore-wo shi-te-mi-mashita ka?	Did he try it?
Sono hito-wa ima sore-wo shi-te-mi-te-i-masu.	He is trying it now.

LESSON 25

The Perfect: "I have done it."

Example:

Watakushi-wa sore-wo shi-te-shimai-mashita.
> *I have done it (I finished doing it).*

The spoken Japanese has no perfect tense, and the verb
shimai (*finish*) is frequently used where perfect forms
would be called for in English:—

Watakushi-wa sore-wo tabe-te-shimai-mashita.
> *I have eaten it up (I ate and finished it).*

Sono hito-wa itte-shimai-mashita.
> *He has gone away.*

Sono hito-wa ki-te-shimai-mashita.
> *He has come already.*

Sono hito-wa suwatte-shimai-mashita.
> *He has sat down already.*

Watakushi-wa sore-wo wasure-te-shimai-mashita.
I have forgotten it.

The above usage of **shimai** reminds us of the peculiar way in which the old Negroes of the southern United States employ the word "done" in their dialect. For instance: "Dey's done gone" (They have gone); "Ah done plum fergit dat" (I have plump forgotten that). I do not know how this usage came into their dialect, but it is most interesting to see that they have a very similar way of thinking and speaking as the Japanese.

Key Words:

-te-shimai-   (*finish*)

Vocabulary:

wasure	*forget*
kowashi	*break*
tsukuri (tsukutte-)	*make*
"**garasu**"	*glass*

Exercises:

Sono hito-wa doko-ni i-masu ka?	Where is he?
Sono hito-wa gakkoo-ni itte-shimai-mashita.	He has gone away to school.
Anata-wa watakushi-wo wa-sure-te-shimai-mashita ka?	Have you forgotten me?
Hai, watakushi-wa anata-wo wasure-te-shimai-mashita.	Yes, I have forgotten you.
Iie, watakushi-wa anata-wo wasure-masen.	No, I do not forget you.

Kore-wa warui inu-de su. Ko-no inu-wa garasu-wo kowa-shi-te-shimai-mashita.

This is a bad dog. This dog has broken up the glass.

Watakushi-wa hako-wo kowa-shi-te-shimai-mashita.

I have broken the box.

Anata-wa hako-wo tsukuri-mashita ka?

Did you make a box?

Anata-wa hako-wo tsukutte-shimai-mashita ka?

Did you finish making the box?

Watakushi-wa kinoo hako-wo tsukuri-mashita.

I made the box yesterday.

Watakushi-wa kinoo hako-wo tsukutte-shimai-mashita.

I finished making the box yesterday.

Watakushi-wa kinoo hako-wo tsukutte-shimai-masen-de-shita.

did not finish making the box yesterday.

Inu-ga pan-wo tabe-te-shimai-mashita.

The dog has eaten up the bread.

Inu-wa pan-wo tabe-te-shimai masen-deshita.

The dog did not eat up the bread.

Kono gohan-wo tabe-te-shi-mai-mashoo.

Let us eat up this rice.

LESSON 26

Review Lesson

Asa-gohan

Vocabulary:

asa-gohan	*breakfast* (**asa** = *morning*)
ikebana	*flower arrangement*
hashi	*chop sticks*
o-wan	*lacquer bowl*
chawan	*rice bowl*
dobin	*tea kettle* (*of earthen ware*)
yunomi	*tea cup*
chabu-dai	*dining table*
o-hitsu	*rice tub*
sara	*tray*

Exercises :

Watakushi-wa asa-gohan-ni pan-wo tabe-masu.

I eat bread at breakfast.

Kono hito-wa asa-gohan-ni Nippon-no mono-wo tabe-te-i-masu.

She is eating Japanese things at breakfast.

Chabu-dai-no ue-ni chawan to dobin to hashi to sara-ga ari-masu.

On the dining table are rice bowls, tea kettle, chop sticks and trays.

Migi-no hito-wa o-wan-no futa-wo totte-i-masu.

The person on the right is taking the lid of the lacquer bowl.

Hidari-no hito-wa chawan-ni gohan-wo totte-i-masu.

The person on the left is taking some rice into the rice bowl.

Dobin-no naka-ni o-cha-ga ari-masu.

There is some tea in the kettle.

Kono hito-wa gohan-wo tabe-te-mi-te-i-masu.

This person is eating and tasting the rice.

Kono hito wa o-wan-no futa-wo totte-mi-te-i-masu.

This person is taking the lid of the bowl to look in.

Migi-no hito-ga dobin to yu-nomi-wo motte-ki-mashita.

The person on the right brought the tea kettle and the cups.

Hidari-no hito-ga o-hitsu-wo motte-ki-mashita.

The person on the left brought the rice tub.

Kore-wa kirei-na heya-desu.

This is a pretty room.

Tokonoma-ni itsumo kakemo-no to ikebana-ga ari-masu.

There are a kakemono and a flower arrangement in the tokonoma always.

Kono hito-wa gohan-no mae-ni niwa-ni itte-ki-mashita.

This person has been to the garden before meal.

Soshite kono hito-wa ikebana-wo tokonoma-ni motte-ki-mashita.	And she brought the flower arrangement to the tokonoma.
Kono hito-wa asa-gohan-wo tabe-te-shimai-mashita.	This person has finished breakfast.
Keredomo sono hito-wa ima tabe-te-i-masu.	But that person is now eating.

LESSON 27

Request: " Will you give me a box ? "

Example:

Hako-wo hitotsu kudasai.

box   one   give

Will you give me one box? (Please give me one box.

The verb **kudasai** is used without **masu.** The subject is usually understood. The numerals (**hitotsu,** etc.) are usually employed adverbially as seen in the example. It is permissible to employ it as adjective to say, " **Hitotsu-no hako-wo kudasai,**" but this sounds affected and is not recommended.

To stress that the box should be given specially to me, one may say:

Watakushi-ni hako-wo hitotsu kudasai.

Will you give one box to me?

The negative request, *Please do not give me a box,* is expressed usually by

Hako-wa iri-masen.   *The box is not needed.*

The verb **kudasai** may be made negative to form an exact equivalent of "do not give me," but the negation without the use of **masu** is beyond our scope now. To say "Do not give me anything," employ **nani-mo**, literally *what-also* or *anything*:

Nani-mo iri-masen.
   Not anything is needed. (*I don't want anything*).

An answer to the request should be:

Hai, age-mashoo.   *Yes, I will give.* (*Yes, let me give.*)
Note that the word for *give* is different in the answer. This is an instance of the Japanese etiquette in speech. The original meaning of the word **age** is to send upward while that of **kudasai** is to send downward. And so the person who requests says politely, "Please send it down to me," and the one who answers says in return, "Yes, I will send it up to you."

The answer in refusal is

Iie, age-rare-masen.   *No, I cannot give you.*

The construction of **age-rare-masen** will be studied in the lesson for Possibility. Until then a student should simply memorize the expression.

Key Words:

-wo	ending for object
-ni	*to*
kudasai	*give*

Vocabulary:

age	*give (upward)*
age-rare	*can give (upward)*
iri	*be needed*
hitotsu	*one*
kippu	*ticket*
nani-mo	*(not) anything*
arigatoo	*thank you*

Exercises:

Nani-wo age-mashoo ka?	What shall I give you?
Kippu-wo hitotsu kudasai.	Will you give me one ticket?
Nan'-no kippu-wo age-mashoo ka?	Ticket for what shall I give you?
Densha-no kippu-wo hitotsu kudasai.	Please give me one street car ticket.
Hai, age-mashoo. Donata-ni age-mashoo ka?	Yes, I will give To whom shall I give it?
Watakushi-ni kudasai. Arigatoo.	Please give it to me. Thank you.
Kono enpitsu-wo kudasai.	Will you give me this pencil?
Iie, age-rare-masen. Pen-wo age-mashoo ka?	No, I cannot give it to you. Shall I give you a pen.
Iie, pen-wa iri-masen. Enpitsu-wo kudasai.	No, I don't want a pen. Give me a pencil.
Age-rare-masen. Pen-wo age-mashoo.	I cannot give you. I will give you a pen.

Donna heya-wo age-mashoo ka?	What kind of a room shall I give you?
Chiisai kirei-na heya-wo kudasai.	Will you give me a small and pretty room?
Chiisai heya-wa ari-masen. Ookii heya-wo age-mashoo.	There is no small room. I will give you a large room.
Ookii heya-wa iri-masen. Chiisai takaku-nai heya-wo kudasai.	I don't want a large room. Give me a small and inexpensive room.
Chiisai heya-wa age-rare masen, keredomo takaku-nai heya-wo age-mashoo.	I cannot give you a small room, but I will give you an inexpensive room.
Arigatoo.	Thank you.
Kono hon-wo age-mashoo ka?	Shall I give you this book?
Iie, iri-masen.	No, I don't need it.
Nani-wo age-mashoo ka?	What shall I give you?
Nani-mo iri-masen.	I don't need anything.

LESSON 28

Request with Verbs: " Will you open it ? "

Examples:

Kore-wo ake-te-kudasai.
  Will you open this? (Please open this.)
Kore-wo ake-nai-de-kudasai.
  Please do not open this.

These are examples of verbs in succession. **Ake-te-ku-dasai** should best be learned as a unit without any reference to English. But if a student finds it easier to learn an expression when there is an English equivalent, it may be suggested that **kudasai** be translated *give the favour of*. Therefore :—

Kore-wo ake-te-kudasai.
> *Give me the favour of opening it.*

Kore-wo ake-nai-de-kudasai.
> *Give me the favour of not opening it.*

The construction of **ake-nai-de-** will be studied later when the inflexion of verbs is taken up.

The answers to the request are :—

Hai, ake-mashoo.
> *Yes, I will open.*

Hai, ake-te-age-mashoo.
> *Yes, I will give you the favour of opening.*
> (respectful)

Iie, ake-rare-masen.
> *No, I cannot open.*

Key Words :

> -te-kudasai
> -nai-de-kudasai

Vocabulary :

> hitotsu   *one*
> hitotsu-mo   *(not) one, (not) any*

futatsu	*two*
mittsu	*three*
yottsu	*four*
itsutsu	*five*
to	*door*
doozo	*please*

Exercises :

To-wo ake-mashoo ka?	Shall I open the door?
To-wo ake-te-age-mashoo ka?	Shall I open the door for you?
Hai, to-wo ake-te-kudasai.	Yes, please open the door.
Nani-wo motte-ki-mashoo ka?	What shall I bring?
Nani-wo motte-ki-te-age-ma-shoo ka?	What shall I bring for you?
O-cha-wo mittsu motte-ki-te-kudasai.	Please bring three teas.
Nani-wo shi-te-age-mashoo ka?	What shall I do for you?
Doozo shinbun-wo yon-de-ku-dasai.	Please read the news-paper.
Hai, yomi-mashoo.	Yes, I will read.
Arigatoo.	Thank you.
Ashita ki-te-age-mashoo ka?	Shall I come tomorrow?
Hai, doozo.	Yes, please.
Sono to-wo futatsu shime-te-kudasai.	Please shut two of those doors.
Iie, shime-rare-masen.	No, I cannot close them.

Doozo kono pan-wo tabe-te-kudasai.	Please eat this bread.
Doozo kono pan-wo tabe-te-shimatte-kudasai.	Please finish up this bread.
Iie, hitotsu-mo tabe-rare ma-sen.	No, I cannot eat any.
Kono hon-wo ima yonde-shi-matte-kudasai.	Will you finish reading this book now?
Hai, soo shi-mashoo.	Yes, I will do so.
Ima densha-ga ari-masen. A-ruite-itte-kudasai.	There is no street car now. Please go on foot.
Soshite kono hako-wo motte-itte-kudasai.	And will you take this box with you?
Kono hako-wa iri-masen. Ko-no hako-wo kowashite-shi-matte-kudasai.	I don't want this box. Please break this box up.
Soshite ookii yoi hako-wo tsukutte-kudasai.	And will you make me a nice big box?

LESSON 29

Numerals (1)

Examples :

Koko-ni hako-ga hitotsu ari-masu.
>   *Here is one box.*

Kore-wa hitotsu-no uchi-de su.
>   *This is one house.*

Kore-wa hitotsu-de-nai uchi-de su.
>   *This is not one house.*

Numerals are noun-adjectives, but they are oftener used adverbially. As it was explained before, it is quite correct to say: " **Koko-ni hitotsu-no hako-ga ari-masu**," but the above way is preferred as more colloquial. There are certain types of expressions in which there is no other way but to use the numerals as noun-adjectives, of which one type of examples are shown above.

Vocabulary :

itsutsu	*five*	**kokonotsu**	*nine*
muttsu	*six*	**too**	*ten*
nanatsu	*seven*	**ikutsu**	*how many ?*
yattsu	*eight*	**takusan**	*many, much*

All the words in the above vocabulary are noun-adjectives. It may be mentioned in passing that the last syllable of the numerals, **tsu**, has a meaning to which the nearest English equivalent is *piece* or *unit*. Also, it must be mentioned that this system of counting goes up to ten only.[1] There is another system of counting which takes care of all numbers.

Exercises :

Kore-wa futatsu-no uchi-de ari-masen.

This is not two houses.

Kore-wa hitotsu-no uchi-de su.

This is one house.

Futatsu-de-nai hon-wo kuda-sai.

Please give me a book which is not in two (volumes).

---

[1] There is a standing riddle for all Japanese children :— " Why does **too** have no **tsu** at its end ?" " Because **itsutsu** has taken an extra **tsu** to itself."

Kono tana-no uē-ni kirei-na sara-ga nanatsu ari-masu.

On this shelf there are seven pretty trays.

Kono yattsu-no hon-wa taisetsu-de ari-masen.

These eight books are not important.

Kono kokonotsu-no hon-wa taisetsu-de su.

These nine books are important.

Anata-wa tegami-wo ikutsu kaki-mashita ka?

How many letters did you write?

Watakushi-wa kinoo tegami-wo yottsu kaki-mashita.

I wrote four letters yesterday.

Anata-wa ima gohan-wo ikutsu tabe-mashita ka?

How many (bowls of) rice did you eat just now?

Watakushi-wa ima gohan-wo mittsu tabe-mashita.

I have just eaten three bowls of rice.

Anata-wa nani-wo ikutsu tabe-mashita ka?

How many of what did you eat?

Watakushi-wa pan-wo futatsu to gohan-wo hitotsu tabe-mashita.

ate two slices of brea and one bowl of rice.

Kono uchi-ni heya-ga takusan ari-masu ka?

Are there many rooms in this house?

Hai, kono uchi-ni heya-ga too ari-masu.

Yes, there are ten rooms in this house.

Anata-wa enpitsu-wo ikutsu motte-ki-mashita ka?

How many pencils did you bring?

Watakushi-wa enpitsu-wo itsutsu motte-ki-mashita.

I brought five pencils.

Ashita gakkoo-ni sandow-itchi-wo takusan motte-iki-mashoo.

Tomorrow let us take many sandwiches to school.

Naifu to fooku-wo takusan motte-ki-te-kudasai.	Please bring many knives and forks.
Ikutsu motte-ki-mashoo ka?	How many shall I bring?
Naifu-wo muttsu to fooku-wo nanatsu motte-ki-te-kuda sai.	Please bring six knives and seven forks.

LESSON 30

Numerals (2)

Examples (1):

Koko-ni hon-ga san-satsu ari-masu.
 Here are three volumes of books.

Koko-ni hon-ga juu-ichi ari-masu
 Here are eleven books.

There are two systems of numerals in Japanese. Here is given the second system:

Vocabulary (1):

ichi	*one*	juu-ichi	*eleven*
ni	*two*	juu-ni	*twelve*
san	*three*	etc.	
shi	*four*	ni-juu	*twenty*
go	*five*	ni-juu-ichi	*twenty-one*
roku	*six*	ni-juu-ni	*twenty-two*
shich	*seven*	etc.	
hach	*eight*	san-juu	*thirty*
ku	*nine*	san-juu-ichi	*thirty-one*
juu	*ten*	etc.	

The numerals of the second system do not have **tsu** for the last syllable. And they need numeral adjuncts, such as **satsu** (*volume*), in indicating the number of things up to ten. One cannot say, **Koko-ni hon-ga san ari-masu**, or **Koko-ni san-no hon-ga ari-masu**. **San** must be followed by **satsu** or other adjuncts according to the kind of things to be numbered. Various kinds of adjuncts are given in the next lesson.

This rule, however, holds with numbers below ten only. The first systems ends at ten and from eleven on there is only the second system which may be used either with or without the adjuncts. Therefore one may say either, **Koko-ni hon-ga juu-ichi ari-masu** or **Koko-ni hon-ga juu-ichi-satsu ari-masu**, or use the numeral as noun-adjective as **juu-ichi-no hon** or **juu-ichi-satsu-no hon**.

The first system is the original Japanese way of counting. In the ancient days it must have been a full system, but since the adoption of the second system from Chinese, the first system beyond ten went into disuse as being less convenient. That is over a thousand years since.

The present Japanese system of numbers above ten is the most logical one possible. By the different combinations of the ten words (from one to ten) all the numbers up to ninety-nine can be expressed.

As the ability to make use of numbers is one of the greatest necessities in travelling in a foreign land, a student is advised to make a complete table of numbers for himself and turn to it every day so as to master them thoroughly.

Vocabulary :

hyaku	*100*
sen	*1,000*
man	*10 000*
juu-man	*100,000*
hyaku-man	*1,000 000*
sen-man	*10 000 000*
oku	*100 000 000*
juu-oku	*1,000 000 000*
hyaku-oku	*10,000,000 000*
sen-oku	*100 000 000 000*
choo	*1,000,000,000,000*
rei	*0*

Examples (2) :

The Japanese numbers should be cut every four places ;
in the following examples it is so done :

go-hyaku san-juu	530
roku-sen go-hyaku san-juu	6530
ni-man roku-sen go-hyaku san-juu	2,6530
ni-hyaku-juu-ni-man roku-sen go-hyaku san-juu	
	212,6530
juu-go-oku ni-hyaku-juu-ni-man roku-sen go-hyaku	
san-juu	15,0212,6530

An easier way of reading a number is, for instance, reading 530 **go-san-rei** or 6530 **roku-go-san-rei**.

Exercises:

Tsukue-no ue-ni ookii hon-ga roku-satsu ari-masu.	There are six big books on the desk.
Kono shichi-satsu-no hon-wa taisetsu-de ari-masen.	These seven books are not important.
Anata-wa tegami-wo ikutsu kaki-mashita ka?	How many letters did you write?
Watakushi-wa kinoo tegami-wo juu-hachi kaki-mashita.	I wrote eighteen letters yesterday.
Anata-wa ima nani-wo ikutsu tabe-mashita ka?	How many of what did you eat just now?
Watakushi-wa ima sandow-itchi-wo juu-ni tabe-mashita.	Just now I ate twelve sandwiches.
Kono uchi-ni heya-ga takusan ari-masu ka?	Are there many rooms in this house?
Hai, kono uchi-ni heya-ga ni-juu ari-masu.	Yes, there are twenty rooms in this house.
Anata-wa enpitsu-wo ikutsu motte-ki-mashita ka?	How many pencils did you bring?
Watakushi-wa enpitsu-wo juu-ku motte-ki-mashita.	I brought nineteen pencils.
Naifu to fooku-wo takusan motte-ki-te-kudasai.	Please bring me lots of knives and forks.
Ikutsu motte-ki-mashoo ka?	How many shall I bring?
Naifu-wo juu-roku to fooku-wo juu-shichi motte-ki-te-kudasai.	Please bring sixteen knives and seventeen forks.
Anata-wa ikutsu-de su ka?	How old are you?
Watakushi-wa kokonotsu-de su.	I am nine.
Sono hito-wa ikutsu-de su ka?	How old is he?
Sono hito-wa shi-juu-go-de su.	He is forty-five.

LESSON 31

Numeral Adjuncts (1)

Examples:

Koko-ni kami-ga ichi-mai ari-masu.
Here is one sheet of paper.

Kore-wo ichi-mai-no kami-ni kaite-kudasai.
Please write this on one sheet of paper.

Vocabulary:

kami	*paper*
mai	*sheet of*
satsu	*volume of*
dai	"*unit,*" used for cars and machinery
hon	"*stick,*" used for long objects as pencils
hiki	"*head,*" used for living things in general
kumi	*set, pair*
hai	—*ful*, as *cupful, spoonful*, etc.

The variety of numeral adjuncts is larger with the Japanese language than with English. They are a kind of words simply troublesome to students with apparently no absolute necessity. In fact it is quite correct to use the first system of the numerals (**hitotsu, futatsu,** etc.) in place of any of the adjuncts, as **Koko-ni kami-ga hito-tsu ari-masu**. Also, there are many things which can not be classified for any one of the adjuncts, such as doors, windows, tables and ink-bottles. Therefore, it may be just as well, and perhaps safer, for a student to use the first system of numerals in all cases. However, one must learn the adjuncts so as to understand them.

There are some euphonic contractions which add to the complication, but that will be taken up in the next lesson. In this lesson all cases of contractions will be carefully avoided.

For making interrogation, such as *how many sheets of* or *how many volumes of,* use **nan-** or **iku-**:

лan-mai	*how many sheets of*
nan-satsu	*how many volumes of*
nan-dai	*how many " units" of*
etc.	
iku-mai	*how many sheets of*
iku-satsu	*how many volumes of*
iku-dai	*how many " units" of*
iku-hon	*how many " sticks" of*
etc.	

The above two groups of words with **nan-** and **iku-** are quite interchangeable, there being no difference in their meaning or uses between them. One may note that **nan-** is abbreviation of **nani** (*what*) and **iku-** is the first two syllables of **ikutsu** (*how many*).

Exercises :

Kami-wo nan-mai age-mashoo ka ?

How many sheets of paper shall I give you ?

Kami-wo roku-mai kudasai.

Please give me six sheets of paper.

Soko-ni hon-ga nan-satsu arimasu ka ?

How many volumes of books are there ?

Koko-ni roku-satsu ari-masu.	Here are six volumes.
Densha-ga ichi-dai ki-mashita.	One street car came.
Anata-wa enpitsu-wo iku-hon motte-ki-mashita ka?	How many pencils did you bring?
Watakushi-wa shichi-hon mo-tte-ki-mashita.	I brought seven.
Niwa-ni inu-ga iku-hiki i-ma-su ka?	How many dogs are there in the yard?
Ni-hiki i-masu.	There are two.
Anata-wa sara to yunomi-wo iku-kumi motte-i-masu ka?	How many sets of trays and cups have you?
Watakushi-wa juu-ni-kumi motte-i-masu.	I have twelve sets.
Gohan-wo takusan tabe-ma-shoo. Anata-wa iku-hai ta-be-masu ka?	Let us eat a lot of rice. How many bowlfuls will you eat?
Watakushi-wa go-hai tabe-mashoo	I will eat five bowlfuls.
Kore-wo ichi-mai-no kami-ni kaki-mashoo ka?	Shall I write this on one sheet of paper?
Iie, kore-wo ni-mai-no kami-ni kaite-kudasai	No, please write it on two sheets of paper.
Ichi-dai-no densha-ni notte-kudasai.	Please get in (ride) one car (together).

LESSON 32

Numeral Adjuncts (2)

Note the following euphonic changes. They are again something troublesome with no absolute necessity. A student who is making a rapid study of the language is advised to pass on quickly to following lessons which contain more useful materials. Numbers themselves are important, but not the adjuncts.

Euphonic Changes:

yo-mai, not shi-mai	*4 sheets*
nana-mai, or sh'chi-mai	*7 sheets*
issatsu	*1 volume*
yon-satsu, or shi-satsu	*4 volumes*
nana-satsu, or shichi-satsu	*7 volumes*
jissatsu	*10 volumes*
juu-issatsu	*11 volumes*
ni-jissatsu	*20 volumes*
yo-dai, not shi-dai	*4 units*
nana-dai, or shichi-dai	*7 units*
ippon	*1 stick*
san-bon	*3 sticks*
yon-hon, or shi-hon	*4 sticks*
roppon	*6 sticks*
nana-hon, or shichi-hon	*7 sticks*
jippon	*10 sticks*
juu-ippon	*11 sticks*
nan-bon	*how many sticks?*

ippiki	*1 head*
san-biki	*3 heads*
yon-hiki, or **shi-hiki**	*4 heads*
roppiki	*6 heads*
nana-hiki, or **shichi-hiki**	*7 heads*
jippiki	*10 heads*
nan-biki	*how many heads?*
ippai	*1 —ful*
san-bai	*3 —fuls*
yon-hai, or **shi-hai**	*4 —fuls*
roppai	*6 —fuls*
nana-hai, or **shichi-hai**	*7 —fuls*
jippai	*10 —fuls*
nan-bai	*how many —fuls?*

kumi is an exception; it has a strange way of counting.

hito-kumi	*1 set*
futa-kumi	*2 sets*
mi-kumi	*3 sets*
yo-kumi	*4 sets*
itsu-kumi	*5 sets*
mu-kumi	*6 sets*
nana-kumi	*7 sets*
ya-kumi	*8 sets*
ku-kumi, or **kyuu-kumi**	*9 sets*
to-kumi	*10 sets*
juu-ichi-kumi	*11 sets*
iku-kumi, or **nan-kumi**	*how many sets?*

The counting of **kumi** is somewhat the mixture of the first and the second systems.

The Japanese people are ever careful to keep the dignity of human beings over the rest of the animal kingdom. Therefore they use a separate system for counting the number of men and women and children.

hitori, or **ichi-nin**	**ku-nin**
futari, or **ni-nin**	**juu-nin**
san-nin	**juu-ichi-nin**
yottari, or **yo-nin**	**juu-ni-nin**
go-nin	**juu-san-nin**
roku-nin	**juu-yo-nin**
nana-nin, or **shichi-nin**	
hachi-nin	**nan-nin ?** or **iku-nin ?**

In recent years the use of **yo** or **yon** instead of **shi**, and **nana** instead of **shichi** has come into general use The reason is that the sound of **shi** and **shichi** are difficult to distinguish especially over the telephone. Needless to say **yo** was borrowed from **yottsu** and **nana** from **nanatsu**

Exercises :

Honbako-ni ookii hon-ga jis-satsu to chiisai hon-ga juu-issatsu ari-masu.

In the bookcase ther. are ten big books and eleven small books.

Shinbun-wo yo-mai katte kudasai.

Please buy four news-papers.

Pen to enpitsu to kami-wo takusan motte-ki-te-kuda-sai.

Please bring me many pens, pencils and pa-pers.

Ikutsu motte-ki-mashoo ka? How many shall I bring?

Pen-wo juu-roppon to enpitsu--wo juu-san-bon to kami-wo ni-juu-yo-mai motte-ki-te-kudasai. Please bring sixteen pens, thirteen pencils and twenty-four sheets of paper.

Soko-ni inu-ga nan-biki i-masu ka? How many dogs are there?

Koko-ni inu-ga ippiki i-masu. There is one dog here.

Mizu-wo nan-bai age-mashoo ka? How many (glasses of) water shall I give you?

San-bai kudasai. Please give me three (glasses).

Anata-wa kono kirei-na sara-wo iku-kumi motte-i-masu ka? How many sets of these pretty trays have you?

Watakushi-wa kono sara-wo itsu-kumi motte-i-masu. have five sets of these trays.

Kono yunomi-wo futa-kumi katte-kudasai. Please buy me two sets of these cups.

Anata-no uchi-ni ima nan-nin-no hito-ga i-masu ka? How many people are there in your house now?

Shichi-nin i-masu. There are seven people.

Nan-de su ka? What is that?

Nana-nin-de su. (The number) is seven.

Soo-de su ka? Is that so? (I see.)

Kono heya-ni hito-ga iku-nin i-masu ka? How many people are there in this room?

Kono heya-ni ima juu-yo-nin i-masu. There are fourteen people in this room now.

LESSON 33

Ordinal Numbers

Examples:

Watakushi-ga ichi-ban-ni ki-mashita.
I came first.

Watakushi-wa ichi-banme-no to-wo ake-mashita.
I opened the first door.

Literally **ichi-ban** means *number one*. When it is used as an adverb, it has the ending **-ni** as in the first of the above examples. When it is used as an adjective as in the second of the examples, it has the ending **-no**. **-Ni** may be remembered as the *in* of *in the first place*, while **-no** may be remembered as the *of* of *of the first place.*

Ichi-ban and **ichi-banme** are almost interchangeable. The latter is more emphatic or precise and tangible, but the distinction is not absolute.

The counting of the ordinal numbers goes **ichi-ban, ni-ban**, etc., quite regularly except for *fourth* which is **yo-ban** and not **shi-ban**. *Fourteenth* is **juu-yo-ban** and all other numbers ending in *four* follow suit.

Key Words:

-ban, -banme	*number (in order)*
-ni	ending for adverbial use *(in)*
-no	ending for adjective use *(of)*

Vocabulary:

nan-ban, nan-banme	*what number? which?*

iku-ban, iku-banme	*what number? which?*
dono (adjective)	*which?*
kodomo	*child*
hikidashi	*drawer*
bangoo	*the number*

Exercises:

Watakushi-ga ichi-ban-ni ki-mashita, soshite anata-ga ni-ban-ni ki-mashita.	I came first and you came second.
Anata-no kodomo-wa dako-ni i-masu ka?	Where is you child?
Watakushi - no kodomo - wa migi - kara roku - banme-ni tatte-i-masu.	My child is standing sixth from the right.
Smith-san-wa doko-ni suwatte-i-masu ka?	Where is Mr. Smith sitting.
Smith-san - wa mae - kara ni-banme hidari-kara go-ban-me-ni suwatte-i-masu.	Mr. Smith is sitting second from the front and fifth from the left.
Kono hito-ga ichi-ban-ni go-han-wo tabe-te shimai- mashita.	This person finished eating the meal first.
Watakushi-ga kono hon-wo ichi-ban-ni yon-de- shimai-mashita.	I finished reading this book first.
Dono heya-ga anata-no-de su ka?	Which room is yours?
San-banme-no heya-ga watakushi-no-de su.	The third room is mine

Nan - banme - no hikidashi-wo ake-mashoo ka?	Which drawer shall I open?
Ue-kara yo-banme-no hikidashi-wo ake-te-kudasai.	Please open the fourth drawer from the top.
Anata-wa nan-ban-de su ka?	What is your number?
Anata-no bangoo-wa nan-de su ka?	What is your number?
Watakushi-wa juu-san-ban-de su.	I am thirteenth.
Kono heya - no bangoo - wa nan-de su ka?	What is the number of this room?
Juu roku-ban-de su.	It is sixteen.
Dore-ga anata-no tsukue-de su ka?	Which is your desk?
Watakushi-no-wa ushiro-kara shichi-banme-de su.	Mine is the seventh from the rear.
Kippu-wa nan-banme-no hikidashi-ni ari-masu ka?	In which drawer is the ticket?
Kippu-wa sono tsukue-no shita-kara ni-banme-no hikidashi-ni ari-masu.	The ticket is in the second drawer from the bottom of that desk.

LESSON 34

Comparison

Examples:

Kono heya-no naka-de watakushi-ga ichi-ban ookiku ari-masu.

In this room I am the biggest.

Watakushi-wa anata yori ookiku ari-masu.

I am bigger than you.

Kono hito-wa watakushi yori motto ookiku ari-masu.

This person is bigger than me.

In Japanese there is no particular words or endings which must be used in comparison, such as *more* and *most*, or —*er* and —*est*. The superlative is expressed simply by the use of **ichi-ban.** In the same way the second biggest, etc., can be expressed by **ni-ban-ni ookiku**, etc. As this is the adverbial use of the numerals, **-ni** should be used as the ending, but with **ichi-ban** it is usually omitted for brevity.

Motto may or may not be used in comparative. Its use makes the statement more definite and emphatic.

Key Words :

-ban	*number* (*in order*)
-no naka-de	*in, among*
-de	*in, among* (abbreviation of **-no naka-de**
motto	*more*
yori	*than*

Vocabulary :

yasui	(regular adjective)	*inexpensive*
hikui	(regular adjective)	*low*
takai	(regular adjective)	*high, expensive*
isu		*chair*

dore	*which one?* (among many)
dochira	*which one?* (of the two)

Exercises :

Kore-wa sore yori takai isu-de su.	This is a more expensive (or higher) chair than that.
Dore-ga ichi-ban yasui isu-de su ka ?	Which is the cheapest chair ?
Kono itsutsu-no isu-no naka-de dore-ga ichi-ban yoi-de shoo ka ?	Of these five chairs which is the best ?
Kore to kore-ga ichi-ban kirei-de su. Kono futatsu-ga yoi-de shoo.	This and this are the prettiest. These two will be good.
Futatsu-wa iri-masen. Sono futatsu-no naka-de dochira-ga yoi-de shoo ka ?	I don't need two. Of those two which is better ?
Kore-wa sore yori yasui isu-de su.	This is a cheaper chair than that.
Yasui mono - wa iri - masen. Takai isu-wo kai-mashoo.	I don't want a cheap thing. I will buy an expensive chair.
Motto takai isu-wa ari-masen ka ?	Isn't there a more expensive chair ?
Kore yori takai mono-wa ari-masen.	There is not anything more expensive than this.
Kono honbako - no naka - de dore-ga ichi-ban yoi hon-de su ka ?	In this bookcase which is the best book ?

Kore-ga ichi-ban yoi hon-de su.	This is the best book.
Sore yori motto yoi hon-wa ari-masen ka?	Isn't there any book better than that?
Kore yori yoi hon-wa ari-masen.	There is no book better than this.
Gakkoo-de donata-ga ichi-ban ookiku ari-masu ka?	Who is the biggest in school?
Watakushi-ga gakkoo-de ichi-ban ookiku ari-masu.	I am the biggest in school.
Gohan-wo motto age-ma-shoo ka?	Shall I give you more rice?
Hai, gohan-wo motto kudasai.	Yes, please give me more rice.

LESSON 35

Time and Money

Examples:

Ima yo-ji shi-fun sugi-de su.
   It is four minutes past four.

Kore-wa yo-yen yon-sen-de su.
   This is four yen four sen.

In the first of the above examples the subject is understood. To be very precise one may say, **jikan-wa ima-yo-ji shi-fun sugi-de su,** (*The time is now four minutes past four.*)

   According to the standard pronunciation of Tokyo

people, **yen** is pronounced **en**, but because of the usage since the early days when Romaji, the Roman way of spelling, was first organized, we are still using the old spelling. The early Romaji spelling was based upon a certain school of thought which insisted on making the pronunciation strong by the use of **y** before e's.

Vocabulary :

ji	*o'clock*
jikan	*hour, time*
nan-ji	*what time?*
fun	*minute*
byoo	*second*
sugi	*past*
mae	*before, ago*
made	*until*
han	*half, half past*
yen	basic unit of Japanese money
sen	one hundredth of one yen
nan-yen	*how many yen?*
nan-sen	*how many sen?*
ikura	*how much?*

Many of the words in the above vocabulary have appeared before in slightly different usages. The following euphonic changes are again the troublesome nonessentials in anguage studies. One can make oneself understood without knowing them. So, the euphonic changes may be taken up according to the degree of zeal and purpose of a student.

Euphonic Changes :

yo-ji (not **shi-ji**)	*4 o'clock*
ippun	*1 minute*
san-pun	*3 minutes*
roppun	*6 minutes*
jippun	*10 minutes*
juu-ippun	*11 minutes*
yo-yen (not **shi-yen**)	*4 yen*
issen	*1 sen*
yon-sen (not **shi-sen**)	*4 sen*
jissen	*10 sen*

Exercises :

Ima nan-ji-de su ka?	What time is it now?
Ima san-ji go-fun sugi-de su.	It is five minutes past three.
Ima juu-ichi-ji juu-go-fun ma-e-de su.	It is fifteen minutes before eleven.
Anata-wa itsu ki-mashita ka?	When did you come?
Watakushi - wa hachi - ji jip-pun-ni ki-mashita.	I came at eight-ten.
Densha-wa nan-ji-ni de-masu ka?	At what time does the electric car go?
Densha-wa yo-ji juu-roppun-ni de-masu.	The electric car goes at 4:16.
Anata-wa itsu kara koko-ni i-masu ka?	Since when have you been here?
Watakushi-wa ni-ji kara ko-ko-ni i-masu.	I have been here since two.

Watakushi-wa ichi-jikan mae kara koko-ni i-masu.	I have been here since one hour ago.
Anata-wa itsu made koko-ni i-masu ka?	Until when will you be here?
Watakushi-wa shichi-ji han made koko-ni i-masu.	I will be here till half past seven.
Gohan-wa nan-ji-de su ka?	What time is the meal?
Gohan-wa juu-ni-ji han-de su.	The meal is half past twelve.
Kore-wa ikura-de su ka?	How much is this?
Kore-wa yo-yen san-jissen-de su.	This is four yen thirty sen.
Densha-no kippu-wa ikura-de su ka?	How much is the electric car ticket?
Shichi-sen-de su.	It is seven sen.
Yokohama made ikura-de su ka?	How much is it to Yokohama?
Yokohama made roku-juu-go sen-de su.	It is 65 sen to Yokohama.
Kono pen to inku-wa ikura-de su ka?	How much are these pen and ink?
Pen-wa yon-sen-de su; inku-wa san-jissen-de su.	The pen is four sen; the ink is thirty sen.
Ichi-ban takai kimono-wa i-kura-de su ka?	How much is the most expensive kimono?
Ni-hyaku go-juu-yen-de su.	It is 250 yen.
Nan-yen-de su ka?	How many yen?
Ni-hyaku go-juu-yen-de su.	Two hundred fifty yen.

LESSON 36

Days, Months, and Years

The Japanese language is very simple in structure and its numerical system is most logical. Only when one wishes to speak idiomatically do the euphonic changes and idiomatic expressions appear here and there to be the seemingly unnecessary bother.

Here are listed all the expressions concerning the counts of the days of a month, of a week, and the months of a year. They make too long and too many lists for one lesson, but they are grouped together for convenience in future references. They are not to be learned at once, and there is not much to be studied about them except simple memorization. A student should give them a quick perusal and pass on to further lessons. But try to return to them now and then for leisurely memorizing.

Days of a Month :

tsuitachi or **ichi-nichi**	*1st*
futsuka or **ni-nichi**	*2nd*
mikka or **san-nichi**	*3rd*
yokka or **yon-nichi**	*4th*
itsuka or **go-nichi**	*5th*
muika or **roku-nichi**	*6th*
nanuka or **shichi-nich**	*7th*
yooka or **hachi-nichi**	*8th*
kokonoka or **ku-nichi**	*9th*

tooka	*10th*
juu-ichi-nichi	*11th*
juu-ni-nichi	*12th*
etc.	
hatsuka	*20th*
nijuu-ichi-nichi	*21st*
misoka	the last day of a month
ganjitsu	*the New Year's Day*

The etymology of the days of a month is very interesting, for it traces its origin to the old lunar calendar, but we shall not go into it. It is a custom in Japan to settle accounts on the last day of every month even when it falls on a Sunday, and **misoka** has become almost a synonym to the pay day. The last day of a year, thirty-first of December, is called **oo-misoka** (great misoka), the most important pay day and no postponement is tolerated—a dreaded day for everybody. But the next day is **ganjitsu,** the New Year's Day. Then all the troubles are forgotten for the day and even the devilish creditors go round smiling.

nan-nichi or **iku-nichi**	*what day? how many days?*
hi	*day*
kyoo or **kon-nichi**	*today*
ashita or **myoo-nichi**	*tomorrow*
kinoo or **saku-jitsu**	*yesterday*

Days of a week :

nichi-yoobi	*Sunday*
getsu-yoobi	*Monday*

ka-yoobi	*Tuesday*
sui-yoobi	*Wednesday*
moku-yoobi	*Thursday*
kin-yoobi	*Friday*
do-yoobi	*Saturday*
nani-yoobi	*what day of the week?*
kon-shuu	*this week*
rai-shuu	*coming week*
sen-shuu	*last week*
shuu-kan	*week,* as **ni-shuu-kan**
	=two weeks

Months of a Year

ichi-gatsu	*January*
ni-gatsu	*February*
san-gatsu	*March*
shi-gatsu	*April*
go-gatsu	*May*
roku-gatsu	*June*
shichi-gatsu	*July*

and so forth regularly to **juu-ni-gatsu,** *December;*

nan-gatsu	*what month?*
nan-ka-getsu	*haw many months?*
ichi-ka-getsu	*one month*
ni-ka-getsu	*two months*
kon-getsu	*this month*
rai-getsu	*next month*
sen-getsu	*last month*
tsuki	*month, moon*

Year

gan-nen	*first year* (of an era)
ich-nen	*first year, one year*
ni-nen	*second year, two years*
san-nen	*third year, three years*
etc.	
kotoshi or **kon-nen**	*this year*
rai-nen or **myoo-nen**	*next year*
kyo-nen or **saku-nen**	*last year*
nan-nen	*what year?*
nan-nen or **iku-nen**	*how many years?*
ichi-ka-nen	*one year*
ni-ka-nen	*two years*
etc.	
toshi	*year*
sai	*years old,* as **ni-sai** = *two years old*

Exercises:

Kyoo-wa nan-nichi-de su ka?	What day (of the month) is (it) today?
Kyoo-wa juu-ni-gatsu ni-juu-go-nichi-de su.	Today is December 25th.
Kyoo-wa nan-no hi-de su ka?	What day is (it) today?
Kyoo-wa Kurisumasu-no hi-de su.	Today is the day of Christmas.
Ashita-wa nani-yoobi-de su ka?	What day of the week is (it) tomorrow?
Ashita-wa ka-yoobi-de su.	Tomorrow is Tuesday.

Anata-wa Nippon-ni nan-nichi i-mashita ka?	How many days were you in Japan?
Watakushi-wa Nippon-ni ni-shuu-kan i-mashita.	I was in Japan for two weeks.
Watakushi-wa Nippon-ni ichi nen to ni-ka-getsu i-mashi-ta.	I was in Japan for one year and two months.
Kono kodomo-wa nan-sai-de su ka?	How old is this child?
Kono kodomo-wa shichi-sai to san-ka-getsu-de su.	This child is seven years and three months.

LESSON 37

Complex Sentences (1)

The House Which I Looked at Was a Very Good house.

Examples:

<u>Watakushi-ga mi-mashita</u> uchi-wa taihen yoi uchi-de shita.

> *The house <u>which I looked at</u> was a very good house.*

<u>Watakushi-ga uchi-ni i-mashita</u> koto-wa yoi koto-de shita.

> *The fact <u>that I was at home</u> was a good thing.*

In the above examples the corresponding portions of the sentences in both Japanese and English are underlined.

One may note (1) that the Japanese language has no relative pronouns such as *which* and *who*; also (2) that all the explanatory words, or subordinate clause, come before the word to be explained. In the first of the above examples **Watakushi-ga mi-mashita** comes before **uchi** while in English *which I saw* comes after *the house*. The same rule holds with the adjectives—an adjective always precedes a noun it modifies. For instance, in Japanese there is no such word order as *a man, good and wise*. It has to be always **yoi rikoo-na hito** (*a good wise man*).

A good way to learn the structure of a Japanese complex sentence is to see how it developed out of the combination of two sentences:

Watakushi-ga <u>uchi-wo</u> **mi-mashita;** <u>sono</u> **uchi-wa yoi uchi-de shita.**

> *I looked at a house; that house was a good house.*

Drop the underlined words and there is the complex sentence. The second sentence of the examples may be considered as a development of the following sentences:—

Watakushi-ga uchi-ni i-mashita; <u>sono</u> **koto-wa yoi koto-de shita.**

> *I was at home; that fact was a good thing.*

Vocabulary:

koto	*fact*
tsukai (tsukatte-i-masu)	*use, employ*
" katarogu "	*catalogue*

Exercises :

Anata ga mi-mashita uchi-wa yoi uchi-de shita ka?	Was the house which you looked at a good house?
Soo-de su, watakushi-ga mi-mashita uchi-wa yoi uchi-de shiat.	Yes, the house I saw was a good house.
Dono hon-wo age-mashoo ka?	Which book shall I give you?
Tana-no ue-ni ari-masu hon-wo kudasai.	Please give me the book which is on the shelf.
Anata-ga motte-i-masu hon-wo kudasai.	Please give me the book which you have.
Anata - ga motte-ki - mashita mono-wa nan-de su ka?	What is the thing which you brought?
Watakushi-ga motte - ki - ma-shita mono-wa hon-no ka-tarogu-de su.	The thing which I brought is a catalogue of books.
Anata-ga sono hon-wo yomi-mashita koto-wa yoi koto-de shita ka?	Was it a good thing that you read that book?
Hai, watakushi-ga kono hon-wo yomi-mashita koto-wa yoi koto-de shita.	That I read this book was a good thing.
Anata-ga tsukatte-i-masu oto-ko-wa yoi hito-de su ka?	Is that man whom you are employing a good person?
Iie watakushi-ga tsukatte-i-masu otoko-wa yoi hito-de ari-masen.	No the man I am employing is not a good person.
Anata-wa itsu kara sono pen-wo motte-i-masu ka?	Since when have you had that pen?

Watakushi-wa kono pen-wo juu-nen mae kara tsukatte-i-masu.

I have been using this pen since ten years ago.

LESSON 38

Complex Sentences (2)

Examples (*1*):

Kore-ga, <u>watakushi-ga kinoo mi-mashita</u>, uchi-de su.

This is the house <u>which I looked at yesterday</u>.

Sono hito-wa " ashita Tokyo-ni iki-mashoo " to ii-mashita.

He said, " Let us go to Tokyo tomorrow."

A subordinate clause may be inserted between the parts of the main clause as seen in the above examples. Because the Japanese language has no relative pronouns, such as *which* or *who*, it is sometimes difficult to know where the subordinate clause begins or ends. The lack of relative pronouns is one of the few, but great, inconveniences of the Japanese language. In this book the subordinate clauses are marked off with commas.

Japanese people are never inconvenienced by the lack of relative pronouns in daily use of the language, but in translating an intricate classical English the Japanese translation is liable to become very involved.

The word **to** in the second sentence of the above

examples is somewhat the equivalent of *that* in English. But **to** is used after all the quotations; and there is no distinction of direct or indirect quotation in Japanese. The quotation mark may or may not be used, and its use causes no difference to the sentence construction.

Example (2):

Hon-wa Eigo-de *book* **to ii-masu.**
   They call **hon** *"book" in English.*

This is an idiomatic expression of peculiar construction. I consider that this sentence was derived from **Hito-wa hon-wo Eigo-de** *book* **to ii-masu,** and that somehow **hon-wo** turned into a subject, **hon-wa.**

Vocabulary:

to	*(that)*
Ei-	*English*
-go	*language*
-de	*in, by means of*
ii (itte-i-masu)	*say, call*
oshie	*teach*
tegami	*letter*

Exercises:

Kore-wa, anata-ga tsukai-ma-shita, hon-de su ka?	Is this the book which you used?
Hai, kore-wa, watakushi-ga tsukai-mashita, hon-de su.	Yes, this is the book which I used.
Kore-wa nan-de su ka?	What is this?

Kore-wa, watakushi-ga kaki-mashita, tegami-de su.	This is a letter which I wrote.
Anata - ga kono tegami - wo kaki-mashita, hito-de su ka?	Are you the person who wrote this letter?
Soo-de su, watakushi-ga, ko-no tegami-wo kaki-mashita, hito-desu.	Yes, I am the person who wrote this letter.
Koko-ni, watakushi-ga Ei-go-de kaki-mashita, tegami-ga ari-masu.	Here is the letter which I wrote in English.
Smith-san-wa, ashita iki-ma-shoo, to ii-mashita ka?	Did Mr. Smith say that he will go tomorrow?
Hai, Smith-san-wa, ashita iki-mashoo, to ii-mashita.	Yes, Smith said that he will go tomorrow.
Soo-de su, Smith-san-wa soo ii-mashita.	Yes, Mr. Smith said so.
Kiyooka-san-wa nan to ii-ma-shita ka?	What did Mr. Kiyooka say?
Kiyooka-san-wa, kono hon-wo motto yonde-kudasai, to ii-mashita.	Mr. Kiyooka said, "Please read this book more."
Tegami-wa Ei-go-de nan to ii-masu ka?	What is tegami called in English?
Tegami-wa Ei-go-de *letter* to ii-masu.	Tegami is called letter in English.
Door-wa Nippon-go-de nan to ii-masu ka? Oshie-te-kuda-sai.	What is door called in Japanese? Please teach me.
Door-wa Nippon-go-de to to ii-masu.	Door is called to in Japanese.

Kodomo-wa doko-ni i-masu ka, to Ei-go-de itte-kudasai.

Will you say in English "Where is the child?"

Kore-wa ikura-de su ka, to Ei-go-de itte-kudasai.

Will you say in English, "How much is this?"

Sono hito-wa, kore-wa juu-go-sen-de su, to ii-mashita.

He said that it was fifteen sen.

LESSON 39

Complex Sentences with When and Where

— kutsu —geta — zoori —

Genkan

Examples :

O-kyaku-ga ki-mashita toki-ni, sono hito-wa uchi-ni
  i-mashita.

> *When the guest came, he was at home.*

Sono hito-ga motte-i-masu mono-wa handobagu-de
  su.

> *That which she is holding is a handbag.*

The above examples may be thought as derived from
the following sentences :—

O-kyaku-ga ki-mashita ; sono toki-ni sono hito-wa
  uchi-ni i-mashita.

> *The guest came; at that time she was at home.*

Sono hito-ga aru mono-wo motte-i-masu ; sono mono-
  wa handobagu-de su.

> *She is holding a certain thing; that thing is
>   a handbag.*

Note that **toki-ni** is not the equivalent of the English
when; **toki-ni** means *at that time,* and the equivalent of
when is simply missing in the Japanese sentence. One
may as well say, **O-kyaku-ga ki-mashita hi-ni, sono
hito-wa uchi-ni i-mashita** (*On the day the guest came,
she was at home*).

Vocabulary :

toki	*time*
tokoro	*place, position*
genkan	*entrance hall*

oku-san	*mistress, wife*
o-kyaku	*guest*
zoori	*sandals*
haki (haite-i-masu)	*put on the feet, wear*
geta	*wooden clogs*
kutsu	*shoes*
ki	*wood, tree*
dan	*steps, stairs*
ishi	*stone*
e	*picture*
tsuitate	*a standing screen*
hairi (haite-i-masu)	*enter*
tori (totte-i-masu)	*take, take off*
sayonara	*good-bye*

Exercises:

Kore-wa rippa-na uchi-no genkan-de su.

> This is the entrance hall of a fine house.

Tatami-ni suwatte-i-masu hito-wa kono uchi-no oku-san-de su.

> The person who is sitting on the tatami is the mistress of the house.

Hidari-ni tatte-i-masu hito-wa o-kyaku-de su.

> The person who is standing on the left is the guest.

O-kyaku-wa zoori-wo haite-i-masu.

> The guest is putting on the sandals.

O-kyaku-ga haite-i-masu mono-wa zoori-de su.

> That which the guest is putting on are the sandals.

Zoori-no hidari-ni ari-masu mono-wa geta-de su.	The things which are at the left of the sandals are the wooden clogs.
Geta-no soba-ni ari-masu mono-wa kutsu-de su.	The things which are at the side of the wooden clogs are the shoes.
Nippon - no hito - wa uchi - ni hairi-masu toki-ni, zoori-wo tori-masu.	When the Japanese people enter a house, they take off the sandals.
Nippon - no hito - wa genkan kara hairi-masu toki-ni, zoori-wo tori-masu;	When the Japanese people enter (a house) through the entrance hall, they take off the sandals.
Soshite uchi kara de-te-iki-masu toki-ni, zoori-wo haki-masu.	And when they go out from the house, they put on the sandals.
Soshite genkan kara de-te-iki-masu toki-ni, zoori-wo haki-masu.	And when they go out of (the house) through the entrance hall, they put on the sandals.
Nippon-no uchi-no naka-wa itsumo kirei-de su.	The inside of a Japanese house is always clean.
Oku-san-no ushiro-ni ari-masu kirei-na e-wa nan-de su ka?	What is that beautiful picture behind the mistress?
Sore-wa tsuitate-no e-de su.	That is the picture on the standing screen.
Kore-wa taihen rippa-na tsuitate-de su.	This is a very fine standing screen.
Tsuitate-ga ari-masu tokoro-wa tatami-no heya-de su.	The place, where the screen is, is a room with reed mats.

O-kyaku-ga tatte-i-masu to-koro-wa ki-no dan-de su.	The place where the guest is standing is a wooden step.
Kutsu to geta to zoori-ga ari-masu tokoro-wa ishi-no dan-de su.	Where the shoes and wooden clogs and sandals are is the stone step.
Ki-no dan-no ue-ni ki-no to-ga ari-masu.	Above the wooden step there are wooden doors.
Oku-san-wa ki-no to-no naka-ni i-masu.	The mistress is inside the wooden doors.
Garasu-no to-ga ishi-no dan-no mae-ni ari-masu.	There is a glass door in front of the stone step.
Keredomo garasu-no to-wa kono e-ni ari-masen.	But the glass door is not in this picture.
Oku-san to o-kyaku-wa sayonara to itte-i-masu.	The mistress and the guest are saying, "Good-bye."
O-kyaku-wa kaeri-masu toki-ni, sayonara to ii-masu.	The guest says "Good-bye" when she goes back.

LESSON 40

Use of Verbs without Masu ; Past

Examples :

Watakushi-ga mi-ta uchi-wa taihen yoi uchi-de shita.

The house which I looked at was a very good house.

O-kyaku-ga ki-ta toki-ni, sono hito-wa uchi-ni i-mashita.

When the guest came, she was in the house.
The auxiliary verb **masu** gives respectfulness to an expression, and its use enables one to employ all verbs without the knowledge of their inflexions. And so I have been able to leave off the study of verbs through quite an advanced lessons in complex sentences.

In actual usage, however, more than one **masu** in a sentence is too cumbersome and sometimes makes it sound excessively polite. And so we will begin with the inflexion of different verbs and learn the expressions more usually employed in daily speech. This does not mean that those sentences in Lessons 37, 38 and 39 are not idiomatic. There is no expression in this book which is not recommended for actual use. There should be at least one **masu** in a sentence usually at the end to give respectfulness.

Let us begin with the Past Forms of a few verbs and their euphonic changes :—

yonda (yomi-ta)	*read*
itta (iki-ta)	*went*
kaetta (kaeri-ta)	*returned*
tsukatta (tsukai-ta)	*used, employed*
kaita (kaki-ta)	*wrote*
shimatta (shimai-ta)	*finished*
kudasatta (kudasari-ta)	*gave*
atta (ari-ta)	*was, were*
mi-ta	*saw*

ake-ta	opened
ki-ta	came
shi-ta	did, played
i-ta	was, were
age-ta	gave
oboe-ta	remembered, learned
oshie-ta	taught

Key Word :

| -ta | verb ending for past |

Vocabulary :

oboe	learn, remember
" tenisu "	tennis
" beesu booru "	base ball
shi	do (play)

Verbs in succession are to be treated as a unit exactly as
when used with **masu**. For instance : **ake-te-mi-ta** (*opened and saw—examined inside*) ; **motte-ki-ta** (*brought*) etc.

Exercises :

Anata-ga motte-ki-ta mono-wa nan-de su ka?	What is the thing which you brought ?
Watakushi-ga motte-ki-ta mo-no-wa kore-de su.	What I brought is this.
Tenisu-wo shi-ta hito-wa do-nata-de su ka?	Who is the person that played tennis ?
Tenisu-wo shi-ta hito-wa wa-takushi-de su.	I am the person who played tennis.

Anata-wa kono to-wo ake-te-mi-mashita ka?	Did you open and look in this door?
Iie, kono to-wo ake-te-mi-ta hito-wa watakushi-de ari-masen.	No, I am not the person who looked in this door.
Watakushi-ga age-ta hon-wa doko-ni ari-masu ka?	Where is the book which I gave (you)?
Anata-ga kudasatta hon-wa koko-ni ari-masu.	The book which you gave me is here.
Koko-ni atta isu-wa doko-ni iki-mashita ka?	Where did the chair, which was here, go?
Niwa-ni i-ta inu-wa doko-ni i-ki-mashita ka?	Where did the dog which was in the yard, go?
Smith-san-wa kinoo Tōkyō-ni itte-ki-ta to ii-mashita.	Mr. Smith said that he made a trip to Tōkyō yesterday.
Smith-wa tegami-wo kaite-shimatta to ii-masu.	Smith says he has finished writing the letter.
Kono-hito-wa Ei-go-wo wasure-te-shimatta to ii-masu.	This man says that he has forgotten English.
Anata-ga beesu-booru-wo shite-i-ta toki-ni, watakushi-wa hon-wo yonde-i-mashita.	When you were playing baseball, I was reading a book.
Watakushi-ga kinoo itta to-koro-wa Tōkyō-de su.	Where I went to yesterday is Tōkyō.
Inu-wa niku-wo tabe-te shi-matta, keredomo gohan-wo tabe-masen-deshita.	The dog ate up the meat, but did not eat the rice.

LESSON 41

Use of Verbs without Masu ; Present

Examples :

Sono hito-ga motte-iru mono-wa handobagu-de su.
The thing which that person is holding is a handbag.

Yomu hon-wo kudasai.
Please give me a book to read.

The Present Form is sometimes called the Infinitive of the Japanese verbs, for as it is seen in the second of the above examples, **yomu hon** may very well be translated *book to read*, although grammatically it is **watakushi-ga yomu hon** (*the book which I should read*) with the subject understood. Also, this Present Form is like the English Infinitive in that it is regularly used in designating a verb ; for instance, we may say " The verb *to read* is **yomu** in Japanese."

There are two types of inflexions among the Japanese verbs besides the irregular. One is that of **yomu** in which the last vowel is **u** for the Present and **i** when followed by -masu or -ta, as **yomi-masu** and **yomi-ta** (**yonda**). The other is that of **iru** which takes **ru** for the Present and nothing when followed by -masu or -ta, as **i-masu** and **i-ta.**

Verbs of Group I

Verb Stem	Present	Past	
yom	yomu	yonda (yomi-ta)	*read*
kak	kaku	kaita (kaki-ta)	*write*
ik	iku	itta (iki-ta)	*go*
kaer	kaeru	kaetta (kaeri-ta)	*return*
hair	hairu	haitta (hairi-ta)	*enter*
tsuka	tsukau	tsukatta (tsukai-ta)	*use*
shima	shimau	shimatta (shimai-ta)	*finish*
kudasar	kudasaru	kudasatta(kudasari-ta)	*give*

Verbs of Group II

Verb Stem	Present	Past	
i	iru	i-ta	*be*
ake	akeru	ake-ta	*open*
mi	miru	mi-ta	*see*
age	ageru	age-ta	*give*
tabe	taberu	tabe-ta	*eat*
oboe	oboeru	oboe-ta	*learn*
oshie	oshieru	oshie-ta	*teach*

Irregular Verbs

Present	Past	
kuru	ki-ta	*come*
suru	shi-ta	*do*
aru	atta (ari-ta)	*be*

The above three are about all the irregular verbs in the whole language. The verb **aru** is irregular in its negative form which will be seen later.

One may inquire how some of the verb stems, e.g. **yom, kak** or **kaer,** are to be pronounced. They are not to be pronounced, and they cannot be written in kana, the Japanese syllabary. I have adopted a new grammar made possible by the use of Romaji, because it makes the explanation of verbs much simpler. Indeed, I believe that Romaji is much more natural and suitable means of writing the Japanese language than the native kana.

Exercises :

Tatami-ni suwatte-iru hito-wa oku-san-de su.	The person who is sitting on the tatami is the mistress.
Hidari-ni tatte-iru hito-wa o-kyaku-de su.	The person standing on the left is the guest.
Geta-no soba-ni aru mono-wa kutsu-de su.	The things which are by the wooden clogs are the shoes.
Nippon-no hito-wa uchi-ni hairu toki-ni, zoori-wo tori-masu ;	Japanese people take off the sandals when they enter a house ;
Soshite uchi kara de-te-iku toki-ni, zoori-wo haki-masu.	And when (they) go out of the house, (they) put on the sandals.
Koko-ni aru mono-wa nan-de su ka?	What is the thing which is here ?
Soko-ni aru mono-wa hako-no futa-de su.	The thing which is there is a lid of a box.
Teeburu-no ue-ni taberu mono-ga ari-masu ka?	Is there (any) thing to eat on the table ?

Iie, taberu mono-wa ari-ma sen.

No, (there) is not (any) thing to eat.

Watakushi-wa kaku toki-ni, itsumo enpitsu-wo tsukai-masu.

When I write, I always use a pencil.

Watakushi-wa Tōkyō-ni iku toki-ni, densha-ni notte-iki-masu.

When I go to Tōkyō, I go in electric car.

LESSON 42

Use of Verbs without Masu ; Future

Example:

Watakushi-wa hon-wo yomoo to omoi-masu.
I think I will read a book.

In the above example one of the two subjects is under-stood. To be grammatically complete it should be : **Watakushi-wa hon-wo yomoo to watakushi-wa omoi-masu.** But it is awkward to repeat a long word like **watakushi** twice in a single sentence.

The use of Future in the Japanese language has been fully explained in Lessons 21 and 22. One may regard that **yomoo** is a shortened form of **yomi-mashoo** with the meaning and uses quite alike.

Verbs of Group I

Verb Stem	Present	Future	
yom	yomu	yomoo	*read*
kak	kaku	kakoo	*write*
ik	iku	ikoo	*go*
kaer	kaeru	kaeroo	*return*
hair	hairu	hairoo	*enter*
tsuka	tsukau	tsukawoo	*use*
shima	shimau	shimawoo	*finish*
kudasar	kudasaru	kudasaroo	*give*
omo	omou	omowoo	*think*
hajimar	hajimaru	hajimaroo	*begin*
asob	asobu	asoboo	*play*
hashir	hashiru	hashiroo	*run*

Verbs of Group II

i	iru	iyoo	*be*
ake	akeru	akeyoo	*open*
mi	miru	miyoo	*see*
age	ageru	ageyoo	*give*
tabe	taberu	tabeyoo	*eat*
oboe	oboeru	oboeyoo	*learn*
oshie	oshieru	oshieyoo	*teach*

Irregular Verbs

	kuru	koyoo	*come*
	suru	shiyoo	*do*
	aru	aroo	*be*

Key Words:

—oo, —woo	Future endings for verbs of Group I
—yoo	Future ending for verbs of Group II

To form Future Form of the verbs of Group I, add **oo** to the stem; when the stem ends in a vowel, use **woo** for euphonic reasons. For the verbs of Group II, add **yoo** to the stem.

Vocabulary:

naka-yoshi	*good friends* (**naka**=*between*, **yoshi** =**yoi**)
kuchi-e	*frontispiece* (**kuchi**=*opening*, **e**= *picture*)
hanashi	*story* (**hanashi-wo suru**=*to tell story*)
omou	*to think*
onna	*woman, female*
onna-no ko	*girl*
otoko-no ko	*boy*
ko	*child*=**kodomo**
hashiru	*to run* (**hashitte-iru**)
hayaku	*early, quick*
hajimaru	*to begin*
asobu	*to play* (**asonde-iru**)

Exercises:

Kono hon-no kuchi-e-wo ake-te-mi-te-kudasai.

Please open and look at the frontispiece of this book.

Watakushi-wa kuchi-e-no hanashi-wo shiyoo to omoi-masu.	I think I will tell the story of (talk about) the frontispiece.
Kore-wa san-nin-no onna-no ko no e-de su.	This is a picture of three girls.
Kore-wa hashitte-iru onna-no ko-no e-de su.	This is a picture of girls who are running.
Kono e-no naka-ni otoko-no ko-wa i-masen.	In this picture there are no boys.
Anata-wa, kodomo-ga hashitte-iru tokoro-wa doko-de aroo to, omoi-masu ka?	Where do you think is the place where the children are running?
Sore-wa gakkoo-no niwa-de su.	That is a school yard.
Kono san-nin-wa naka-yoshi-de su.	These three are good friends.
Kono gakkoo-no onna-no ko-wa itsumo naka-yoshi-de su.	The girls of this school are always good friends.
Hidari-ni iru ko-ga "sono ki made hashiroo" to ii-mashita.	The child who is on the left said, "Let us run to that tree."
Migi-no ko-ga ichi-ban mae-ni hashitte-i-masu.	The child on the right is running foremost.
Ichi-ban migi-ni iru ko-ga ichi-ban chiisaku aroo to omoi-masu.	(I) think that the child who is on the extreme right is the smallest.
Nippon-no kodomo-wa asa hayaku gakkoo-ni iki-masu;	The Japanese children go to school early in the morning;
Soshite gakkoo-ga hajimaru mae-ni asobi-masu.	And before the school begins (they) play.

Gakkoo-ga hajimaru jikan-wa hachi-ji-de su.	The time when the school begins is eight o'clock.
Keredomo shichi-ji mae-ni takusan-no kodomo-ga gakkoo-ni ki-te-asonde-i-masu.	But before seven o'clock many children come and are playing at school.
Asa hayaku asobu koto-wa yoi koto-de su.	To play early in the morning is a good thing.
Watakushi-wa ashita-no asa shichi-ji-ni gakkoo-ni itte-miyoo to omoi-masu.	I think I will go to school and see at seven o'clock tomorrow morning.
Soshite asonde-iru kodomo-wo miyoo to omoi-masu.	And I think I will watch the children who are playing.

LESSON 43

Present Negative without Masu

Examples:

Sore-wo ake-nai-de kudasai.
Please do not open that.

Watakushi-wa moo gakkoo-ni ika-nai to ii-mashita.
I said that I do not go to school any more.

Key Words:

—a	ending for verbs of Group I
-nai	*not, do not*

To form Present Negative the verbs of Group I takes the ending **a** and the auxilliary verb **-nai** is attached to it. When the stem ends in a vowel, the euphony requires **a** to be **wa**. For verbs of Group II **-nai** is attached directly to the verb stem.

Refer to Lesson 28 where we first had **Ake-nai-de-kudasai.** The connective **-de** is a euphonic variation of **-te**. It is easier to pronounce **nai-de** than **nai-te**.

With the use of **-nai** one can form a larger variety of verbs in succession :

motte-ko-nai	*do not bring*
mota-nai-de-kuru	*come without carrying*
shi-te-mi-nai	*do not try*
shi-nai-de-miru	*do not do and see* (*see what it will be like if one does not do*)
shi-te-i-nai	*be not doing*
shi-nai-de-iru	*do not do and be* (*stay inactive*)
etc.	

In Lesson 27, *Please do not give me a book* was left off, because the negation without the use of **masu** was beyond our scope then. Now it can be shown :

Hon-wo kudasara-nai-de-kudasai.

> *Please do not give me the book* (*Give me the favour of not giving the book*).

This is a cumbersome expression, but cumbersomeness itself implies politeness and conveys respect.

Verbs of Group I

Verb Stem	Present	Present Negative	
yom	yomu	yoma-nai	*read*
kak	kaku	kaka-nai	*write*
ik	iku	ika-nai	*go*
kaer	kaeru	kaera-nai	*return*
hair	hairu	haira-nai	*enter*
tsuka	tsukau	tsukawa-nai	*use*
shima	shimau	shimawa-nai	*finish*
kudasar	kudasaru	kudasara-nai	*give*
omo	omou	omowa-nai	*think*
hajimar	hajimaru	hajimara-nai	*begin*
asob	asobu	asoba-nai	*play*
hashir	hashiru	hashira-nai	*run*

Verbs of Group II

i	iru	i-nai	*be*
ake	akeru	ake-nai	*open*
mi	miru	mi-nai	*see*
age	ageru	age-nai	*give*
tabe	taberu	tabe-nai	*eat*
oboe	oboeru	oboe-nai	*learn*
oshie	oshieru	oshie-nai	*teach*

Irregular Verbs

	kuru	ko-nai	*come*
	suru	shi-nai	*do*
	aru	nai	*be*

Note the peculiar irregularity of the verb **aru**.

Vocabulary :

| moo | *already, any more* |
| mada | *yet* |

Exercises :

Koko-ni takai hon-wa nai, keredomo yasui hon-wa arimasu.

There is no expensive books here, but there are some cheap books.

Watakushi-wa mada kyoo-no shinbun-wo yoma-nai, keredomo anata-wa yomi-mashita ka?

I have not read today's newspaper, but did you read (it)?

Watakushi-wa moo yomi-mashita.

I have already read (it).

Kore-wa taisetsu-na hon-de nai, keredomo anata-wa ka-woo to omoi-masu ka?

This is not an important book, but do you think you will buy it?

Kono shinbun-wo yonde-age-mashoo ka?

Shall I read this newspaper for you?

Iie, yoma-nai-de-kudasai.

No, please do not read it.

Sono hito-wa mada heya-ni iru to omoi-masu ka?

Do you think he is still in the room?

Sono hito-wa moo i-nai to omoi-masu.

I think he is not (there) any more.

Gakkoo-wa mada hajimari-masen ka?

Hasn't the school begun yet?

Gakkoo-wa mada hajimara-nai to omoi-masu.

I think the school has not begun yet.

Gakkoo-wa moo hajimatta to omoi-masu.

I think the school has begun already.

Anata-wa hon-wo motte-ko-nai to ii-mashita ka?

Did you say that you did not bring the books?

Soo-de su.

Yes.

Gakkoo-ni hon-wo mota-nai-de-kuru koto-wa yoku-nai koto-de su.

To come to school without carrying the books is not good.

Moo san-ji-de su. Gakkoo-ni mada kodomo-ga iru to omoi-masu ka?

It is already three o'clock. Do you think the child is still at the school?

Kodomo-wa moo i-nai to o-moi-masu.

I think the child is not there any more.

LESSON 44

Past Negative and Future Negative

Examples:

Sono hito-wa Tōkyō-ni ika-nakatta to ii-masu.
He says he did not go to Tōkyō.

Sono hito-wa Tōkyō-ni ika-nakaroo to omi-masu.
I think he will not go to Tōkyō.

Exactly as was with the Present Negative, the Past and Future Negatives are formed by adding **nakatta** or **nakaroo** to the **a** (or **wa**) ending of the verbs of Group I and to the stem of those of Group II.

Verbs of Group I

Verb Stem	Past Negative	Future Negative	
yom	yoma-nakatta	yoma-nakaroo	*read*

kak	kaka-nakatta	kaka-nakaroo	*write*
ik	ika-nakatta	ika-nakaroo	*go*
kaer	kaera-nakatta	kaera-nakaroo	*return*
hair	haira-nakatta	haira-nakaroo	*enter*
tsuka	tsukawa-nakatta	tsukawa-nakaroo	*use*
shima	shimawa-nakatta	shimawa-nakaroo	*finish*
kudasa	kudasara-nakatta	kudasara-nakaroo	*give*
omo	omowa-nakatta	omowa-nakaroo	*think*

Verbs of Group II

i	i-nakatta	i-nakaroo	*be*
ake	ake-nakatta	ake-nakaroo	*open*
mi	mi-nakatta	mi-nakaroo	*see*
age	age-nakatta	age-nakaroo	*give*
tabe	tabe-nakatta	tabe-nakaroo	*eat*
oboe	oboe-nakatta	oboe-nakaroo	*learn*
oshie	oshie-nakatta	oshie-nakaroo	*teach*

Irregular Verbs

	ko-nakatta	ko-nakaroo	*come*
	shi-nakatta	shi-nakaroo	*do*
	nakatta	nakaroo	*be*

Vocabulary :

" bisuketto "	*biscuits*
sukoshi	*a little, a few, some*
sukoshi-mo	*(not) any*
okashi	*sweets, confectionery*

Sukoshi, which in its proper sense means *little* or *few* is generally used for *some* although there is a proper word for *some—**ikuraka.*** This is another example of Japanese politeness in speech. One would never say, "Please give me some biscuits;" One would say, "Please give me a few biscuits" (**Bisuketto-wo sukoshi kudasai.)**

Exercises :

Todana-ni taberu mono-ga ari-masu ka?	Is there anything to eat in the cupboard?
Todana-ni taberu mono-wa nakaroo to omoi-ma su.	I think there is not anything to eat in the cupboard.
Kinoo bisuketto-ga takusan atta to omoi-masu	I think there were many biscuits yesterday.
Ima sukoshi-mo nakaroo to omoi-masu.	I think there is not any now.
Bisuketto-ga hitotsu-mo ari-masen ka?	Isn't there (even) one biscuit?
Hitotsu-mo ari-masen. Kinoo kodomo-ga tabe-te-shimai-mashita.	There is not even one. The children ate them up yesterday.
Kodomo-wa tabe-nakatta to ii-masu.	The children say they did not eat.
Kodomo-wa soo takusan tabe-nakaroo to omoi-masu.	I think the children will not eat so much.
Keredomo ima kono todana-ni bisuketto-wa sukoshi-mo ari-masen.	But now in this cupboard there is not any biscuits.

Nippon-no okashi-wa ari-masen ka?

Isn't there any Japanese cakes?

Hai, Nippon-no okashi-wa takusan ari-masu.

Yes, there are plenty of Japanese cakes.

Kodomo-ga kaeru mae-ni sono okashi-wo tabe-mashoo

Let us eat those cakes before the children come back.

Kodomo-wa kinoo hayaku kaera - nakatta, keredomo kyoo hayaku kaeroo to o-moi-masu.

The children did not come back early yesterday, but I think they will come back early today.

Anata-wa kore-wo tabe-te-mimashita ka?

Did you try this?

Iie, watakushi-wa mada sore-wo tabe-nakatta to omoi-masu.

No, I think I have not eaten that yet.

Anata-ga taberu mae-ni sore-wo sukoshi kudasai.

Please give me some of that before you eat.

Kono okashi-wo mada age-nakatta to omoi-masu; sukoshi age-mashoo ka?

I think I have not given (you) this cake yet; shall I give you some?

Mada kudasara - nakatta to omoi-masu. Sukoshi kudasai.

I think (you) have not given me (it) yet. Please give me some.

LESSON 45

Inflexion of Verbs

Let us tabulate all the different forms of verbs we have so far studied, and we shall see the inflexion of Japanese verbs.

Inflexion of Yomu, a Verb of Group I

Verb Stem	Verb Ending	Words that Follow
yom	a (wa)	nai nakatta nakaroo *and inflexions of* **Nai**
	i	masu mashita mashoo ta te-iru *and verbs, auxiliary verbs, adverbs*
	u	oki hito *and nouns and pronouns. Also this ending may end a sentence.*
	e	(command)
	oo (woo)	(future)

Japanese verbs do not inflect according to tense and mood or voice as all the European verbs do though they fulfil the same purpose. The Japanese verbs inflect according to the words that follow them. And those of Group I have five endings which happen to be the five letters of the vowels.

The first ending **a** is used when the negative words follow, as **yoma-nai,** etc. If the verb stem ends in **a** vowel, **wa** is employed, as **omowa-nai**.

The second ending **i** is used when "operative" words such as verbs, auxiliary verbs, or adverbs follow, as **yomi-masu**, **yomi-ta** (**yonda**), **yonde-iru**, etc. An example of an adverb following, which we have not had, is **yomi-nagara** (*while reading*).

The third ending **u** is used when nouns follow or when there is no word to follow and sentence ends, as **yomu hito** (*a man to read*) or **Watakushi-ga yomu** (*I read*).

The fourth ending **e** is imperative, or command, which may be used in a quotation, as **Sono hito-wa "Kore-wo yome" to ii-mashita**, (*He said, "Read this."*) This type of sentences has not been taken up so far, because in actual usage a request—**kudasai**—is preferred to a command.

The fifth and the last ending **oo** (or **woo**) is Future. Its use is quite like the third ending **u**; it may be followed by nouns or it may end a sentence.

Inflexion of Akeru, a Verb of Group II

Verb Stem	Verb Ending	Words that Follow
	—	nai
		nakatta
		nakaroo
		and inflexion of **Nai**
		masu
		mashita
ake	—	mashoo

$$
\left.\begin{array}{l}
\text{ta} \\
\text{te-iru} \\
\quad \textit{and verbs, auxiliary} \\
\quad \textit{verbs, adverbs}
\end{array}\right\}
$$

$$
\text{ru} \left\{\begin{array}{l}
\text{toki} \\
\text{hito} \\
\quad \textit{and nouns and pro-} \\
\quad \textit{nouns. Also this ending} \\
\quad \textit{may end a sentence.}
\end{array}\right.
$$

ro   (command)

yoo   (future)

The verbs of Group II lack the first two of the endings, and the words that follow are attached directly to the verb stem. Otherwise the usage is quite like that of the verbs of Group I.

The three irregular verbs, which change the stem as well as the endings, go through the inflexions as follows:

ko-	ki-	kuru	koi	koyoo	*come*
shi-	shi-	suru	shiro	shiyoo	*do*
—	ari-	aru	are	aroo	*be*

The peculiarity of *aru* is that its negative forms are simply *nai, nakatta, nakaroo* etc. (is not, was not, will not be, etc.) without the stem or ending usual with all other verbs. Otherwise *aru* is quite regular in its inflexion.

In writing these lessons the writer endeavoured

most to make things simple and clear. He is quite aware that the above inflexions of verbs do not conform exactly to the etymological grammar of the Japanese language. Those students who advance into the studies of classical Japanese, or those who look into the traditional grammar, will find that the verbs should have six endings instead of five and that the Future Form do not belong where it is seen in the above tables. However, the above tables are correct as far as the spoken language is concerned. This is mentioned simply for the purpose of telling that the Japanese was once a very complicated language which in course of time simplified itself, and that there still remain a good deal of undigested inconsistencies.

This writer has a certain idea in spelling the Romaji according to the usage of kana so as to maintain a connection between the spoken and the classical Japanese. For instance, the Future Ending may be spelled **au,** as **yomau** and pronounced **yomoo.** This will simplify the subsequent study of kana and their uses, and also the more advanced studies in the classical Japanese. But the idea is not yet ripe, and he has decided to spell the Romaji of this book according to the pronunciation.

The inflexion of the verb **tatsu** which belongs to Group I goes as follows:

tata· tachi- tatsu tate tatoo *stand*

This apparent irregularity is due to the pronunciation of the Japanese. Refer to the table of Fifty Basic

Sounds in Japanese Writing and Pronunciation of the Appendices (P. 172). You will find that the column of **ta** goes **ta chi tsu te to.** The Japanese language do not have the sounds of **ti** or **tu,** and they are replaced by **chi** and **tsu.** Therefore, to the Japanese the verb **tatsu** is not irregular at all. There are several instances of this sort.

There is no particular way for a student to tell which group of inflexion a Japanese verb belongs to except looking up in a dictionary. In this book all the verbs in the Vocabulary in the Appendices are indicated by the Roman numerals.

LESSON 46
Review Lesson

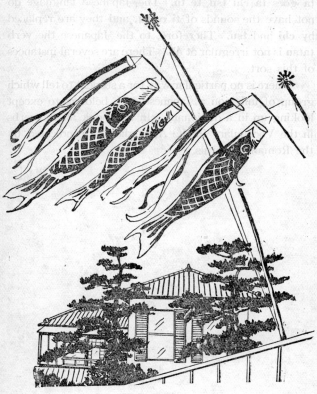

Koi-nobori

Vocabulary:

koi-nobori   *carp streamer* (**koi**=*carp*)

ageru	*to raise, to send up* (verb of Group II.)
omatsuri	*festival*
musha-ningyoo	*warrior dolls* (**musha** = *warrior*)
oku	*to place* (verb of Group I)
tsuyoi	*strong* (regular adjective)
sakana	*fish*
naru	*to become, to grow* (verb of Group I)
matsu	*pine*
tonari-no	*neighbouring* (noun-adjective)

Exercises :

Kore-wa koi-nobori-no e-de su.	This is the picture of carp streamers.
Koi-nobori-wo ageru hi-wa Go-Gatsu Itsuka-de su.	The day when (they) raise the carp streamers is May fifth.
Go-Gatsu Itsuka-wa otoko-no ko-no omatsuri-no hi-de su.	May fifth is the day of festival for boys.
Kodomo-wa tokonoma-ni musha-ningyoo-wo oki-masu ;	The children place the warrior dolls in the alcove ;
Soshite niwa-ni koi-nobori-wo age-masu.	And raise the carp streamers in the yard.
Koi-wa tsuyoi sakana-de su.	Carp is a strong fish.
Kodomo-wa koi-nobori-wo miru toki-ni tsuyoku naroo to omoi-masu.	When the children look at the carp streamers they think they will grow strong.

Kodomo-wa musha-ningyoo-wo miru toki-ni tsuyoi hito ni naroo to omoi-masu.

When the children look at the Warrior dolls, they think they will become strong men.

Kono shashin-no koi-nobori-no shita-ni aru ki-wa matsu-no ki-de su.

The tree which are under the carp streamers of this photograph are pine trees.

Nippon-no matsu-no ki-wa taihen rippa-de su.

The Japanese pines are very fine.

Nippon-no matsu-no ki yori rippa-na ki-ga aroo to omoi-masu ka?

Do you think there is a tree finer than the Japanese pine?

Kono uchi-ni otoko-no ko-ga futari i-masu.

In this house there are two boys.

Kono uchi-no hito-wa koi-no-bori-wo futatsu age-mashi-ta.

The people of this house raised two carp streamers.

Ue-no koi-wa ookii ko-no-de shoo, soshite shita-no chii-sai koi-wa chiisai ko-no-de shoo.

The upper carp is probably for the bigger boy, and the lower, smaller carp is for the little boy.

Migi-ni aru koi-wa tonari-no uchi-no-de su.

The carp on the right is of the neighbouring house.

Tonari-no hito-wa kyonen koi-wo age-nakatta, keredo-mo kotoshi age mashita.

The people of the next door did not raise the carp last year, but this year they did.

Kodomo-wa Go-Gatsu Itsuka-ni yoi mono-wo takusan tabe-te-asobi-masu.

On May fifth children eat a great deal of good things and play.

Go-Gatsu Itsuka-wa yoi hi-de su.

The Fifth of May is a good day.

LESSON   47

Possibility : " I can read it." (1)

Examples:

Watakushi-ni sore-ga yom-are-masu.
I can read it (It is readable to me.)

Watakushi-ni sore-ga tabe-rare-masu.
I can eat it.

Key Words :

-ni	*to* (used after the person or thing which acts)
-ga, -wa	used after the thing or person who receives the action
-are-	*can* (used after the verbs of Group I)
-rare-	*can* (used after the verbs of Group II)

-Are and **-rare** are auxiliary verbs. Both are attached to the verb stems, and they have inflexion quite similar to that of the verbs of Group II.

ending	words that follow
—	⎧ nai
	⎪ nakatta
	⎨ nakaroo
	⎩ *and inflexion of* **Nai**
yom-are-	⎧ masu
tabe-rare- —	⎪ mashita
tsuka-ware-	⎨ mashoo
	⎩ masen

ta

-te-iru

*and verbs, auxiliary
verbs, adverbs*

toki

hito

ru

*and nouns. Also this
ending may end a sen-
tence.*

ro   (command)

yoo   (future)

When the verbs of Group I ends in a vowel, **-wareru**
instead of **-areru** is used, as **tsuka-wareru** (*can use*),
shima-wareru (*can finish*), etc.

As for the irregular verbs, they are as follows:

ko-rareru	*can come*
se-rareru or **shi-rareru**	*can do*
ar-areru	*can be*

Japanese is what is termed an agglutinative language, that is to say, it builds its words and grammatical
forms by means of suffixes attached one after another
to a stem. In fact a verb can have a long trail of suffixes and auxiliary verbs after it, reaching to the other
end of a line. For instance:

**Watakushi-wa sono toki sore-wo yonde-mi-te-i-rare-
masen-deshita.**

> (*At that time I could not be reading and examin-
> ing it.*)

Here is an expression without a subject:

Watakushi-ni ik-are-masu. *I can go.*

Here we see that sometimes a Japanese sentence is constructed without a subject. In fact, to a Japanese mind a subject in the sense of the European grammar is not a necessity. Also, -wa and -ga are not strictly the endings for the subject; they often serve as endings of emphasis. It is quite usual, though erroneous, to say: **Watakushi-wa ik-are-masu** (*I can go*), or **Watakushi-wa kore-ga yom-are-masu** (*I can read this*). This second sentence employs both -wa and -ga in a single sentence, but it sounds quite natural to a Japanese ear.

It is better for a student to learn the most correct and logical expressions in the beginning. And so, in these lessons all sentences which appear ungrammatical to a European mind will be avoided. A student, however, should be forewarned of a few peculiarities of the Japanese language.

Vocabulary :

hanasu	*to speak, to tell* (Group II)
sugu	*at once*
kara	*therefore, because*

Exercises :

Anata-ni Ei-go-ga hanas-are-masu ka ?	Can you speak English ?
Hai, watakushi-ni Ei-go-ga hanas-are-masu.	Yes, I can speak English.

Anata-ni sugu ko-rare-masu ka?	Can you come at once?
Hai, ik-are-masu. Sugu iki-mashoo.	Yes, I can go. I will go at once.
Iie, Watakushi-wa gakkoo-ni iki-masu kara ima anata-no uchi-ni ik-are-masen.	No, I go to school, and so I cannot go to your house now.
Anata-wa kono hon-wo kyoo yonde-shima-ware-masu ka?	Can you finish reading this book today?
Kyoo watakushi-wa Yokoha-ma-ni iki-masu kara kono hon-wo yonde-i-rare-nai to omoi-masu.	Today I go to Yokoha-ma, therefore I think I cannot be reading this book.
Keredomo ashita yonde-shi-ma-ware-yoo to omoi-ma-su.	But I think I can finish reading it tomorrow.
Watakushi-ni kono to-ga ake-rare-masen; anata-ni ake-rare-masu ka?	I cannot open this door; can you open it.
Hai, ake-rare-yoo to omoi-ma-su.	Yes, I think I can open it.
Kore-wa taihen ookii hako-de su keredomo anata-ni mot-te-ik-are-masu ka?	This is a very large box but can you carry it away?
Hai, motte-ik-are-mashoo.	Yes, I (probably) can.
Anata-wa koko-ni juu-ni-ji made i-rare-masu ka?	Can you be here till twelve o'clock?
Hai, i-rare-masu.	Yes, I can.
Sono hon-wo kudasai.	Please give me that book.
Kono hon-wa age-rare-masen.	I cannot give you this book.

LESSON 48
Possibility: "I can read it" (2)

Examples:

Watakushi-ni sore-ga deki-masu.
>*I can do it.*

Watakushi-ni sore-wo yomu koto-ga deki-masu.
>*I can read it. (To read is possible to me.)*

Key Words:

-ni	*to*
koto-ga	*(that)*
dekiru	*to be possible* (Verb of Group II)

Here is the second way to express Possibility. The two ways are employed quite indiscriminately, **yom-areru** and **yomu koto-ga dekiru** having practically the same sense and meanings. **Dekiru** is a verb and unlike the auxiliary verbs, **-are** and **-rare,** it is used independently

Exercises:

Anata-ni Ei-go-ga deki-masu ka?	Can you (speak) English?
Hai, deki-masu.	Yes, I can.
Anata-ni sugu kuru koto-ga deki-masu ka?	Can you come at once?
Hai, iku koto-ga deki-masu. Sugu iki-mashoo.	Yes, I can go. I will go at once.

Iie, watakushi-wa gakkoo-ni iki-masu kara ima anata-no uchi-ni iku koto-wa deki-masen

No, I go to school, and so I cannot go to your house now.

Anata-wa kono hon-wo kyoo yonde-shimau koto-ga deki-masu ka?

Can you finish reading this book today?

Kyoo watakushi-wa Yokohama-ni iki-masu kara kono hon-wo yonde-iru koto-wa deki-nai to omoi-masu.

Today I go to Yokohama, therefore I think I cannot be reading this book.

Keredomo ashita yonde-shimau koto-ga deki-yoo to o-moi-masu.

But I think I can finish reading it tomorrow

Watakushi-ni kono to-wo ake-ru koto-ga deki-masen; anata-ni deki-masu ka?

I cannot open this door; can you?

Hai, deki-yoo to omoi-masu.

Yes, I think I can.

Kore-wa taihen ookii hako-desu keredomo anata-ni motte-iku koto-ga deki-masu ka?

This is a very large box, but can you carry it away?

Hai, deki-mashoo.

Yes, (probably) I can.

Anata-ni koko-ni juu-ni-ji-made iru koto-ga deki-masu ka?

Can you be here till twelve o'clock?

Hai, iru koto-ga deki-masu.

Yes, I can be (here).

Sono hon-wo kudasai.

Please give me that book.

Kono hon-wa ageru koto-ga deki-masen.

I cannot give you this book.

LESSON 49

Passive Voice

Example:

Tori-ga inu-ni tor-are-mashita.
The bird was taken (caught) by the dog.

Key Words:

-ga, -wa	ending for subject, one who receives the action
-ni	*by*, ending for one who acts
-areru	passive auxiliary verb used after verbs of Group I
-rareru	passive auxiliary verb used after verbs of Group II

It is very strange, but interesting, to see that the Passive Form and Possibility employ quite the same words and construction. It is not impossible to take the above example to mean "The dog was able to catch the bird." **Watakushi-ni kore-ga yom-are-masu** can mean *I can read this* quite as well as *This is read by me*. **Kore-ga** may be placed before **Watakushi-ni** without any change in the meaning except emphasis.

However, no Japanese feel any inconvenience, for after all how much difference is there between *It is readable to me* and *It is read by me* when both are boiled down to their barest essence of meaning? Besides, some other verbs are usually employed along with the

Passive Form to make it easier to distinguish them.
For instance:

Tori-ga inu-ni tor-are-te-shimai-mashita.
The bird had been caught by the dog.

This sentence cannot possibly mean, "The dog was
able to catch the bird."

Vocabulary:

sensei	*teacher;* also used as a title
komaru	*to be troubled* (verb of Group I)
moo hitotsu	*one more, another*
kowasu	*to break* (verb of Group I)
tsukuru	*to make* (verb of Group I)

Exercises:

Kono hon-wa takusan-no hi-to-ni yom-are-mashita.	This book has been read by many people.
Watakushi-wa Smith Sensei-ni Ei-go-wo oshie-rare-ma-shita.	I was taught English by Prof. Smith.
Watakushi-wa, chiisaku atta toki-ni, kono hon-wo oshie-rare-mashita.	When I was little, I was taught this book.
Watakushi-wa, chiisaku atta toki-ni, Ei-go-wo oshie-rare-nakatta kara, ima komatte-i-masu.	Because I was not taught English when I was little, I am much troubled now.
Kono hon-wa takusan-no hi-to-ni yom-are-te-i-masu.	This book is being read by many people.

Ima ichi-ban takusan yom-are-te-iru hon-wa nan-de su ka?

What is the book which is read most (widely) now?

Anata-no uchi-wa koko kara mi-rare-masu ka?

Is your house seen from here? (Can one see your house from here?)

Hai, koko kara mi-rare-masu.

Yes, it is seen from here. (One can see it from here.)

Kono hako-wa kodomo-ni ko-was-are-te - shimai - mashita kara moo hitotsu tsukutte-kudasai.

This box was broken by the child, so please make another.

Kinoo mado garasu-ga ichi-mai kowas-are-mashita, so-shite kyoo moo ichi-mai kowas-are-mashita.

Yesterday one window glass was broken, and today one more was broken.

LESSON 50

Causative: " I make him go "

Examples:

Watakushi-wa kodomo-wo gakkoo-ni ik-ase-masu.
 I let the child go to school.

Watakushi-wa kodomo-ni gohan-wo tabe-sase-masu.
 I let the child eat some rice.

Key Words:

-wa   ending for person or thing which causes the action

-wo	ending for person or thing which receives the action
-ni	ending for person or thing which is caused to act
-aseru	*let* auxiliary verb for Causative used after verbs of Group I
-saseru	*let* auxiliary verb for Causative used after verbs of Group II

The auxiliary verbs **-aseru** and **-saseru** are very much like **-areru** and **-rareru** in their uses and inflexions.

Ending	Words that Follow
—	nai nakatta nakaroo *and inflexion of* Nai
ik-ase tabe-sase → tsuka-wase	masu mashita mashoo ta te-i-masu *and negative forms of masu, verbs, auxiliary verbs, adverbs*
ru	toki hito *and nouns. Also this ending may end a sentence.*
ro	(command)

yoo   (future)

Irregular verbs take the Causative as follows:

ko-saseru   *to let someone come*

saseru   *to let someone do*

ar-aseru   *to let someone be*

In fact the Causative form of the verb **suru** is the original of the Causative Auxiliary Verbs.

Let us examine some examples in which **saseru** and **-rareru** are used together:

Kodomo-wa   okusan-ni   gohan-wo   tabe-sase-rare-mashita.

The child was forced to eat the meal by the mistress (though he was not hungry.)

This is a rather poor one, but it is meant to be an example of a Passive Causative. The combination in reverse order—Causative Passive—will be **tabe-rare-sase-ru** (*to cause something to be eaten*). A case for this latter combination would be rather rare except for such as causing a mouse to be devoured by a cat. Putting the case in the view point of mouse, this again can be made passive as **tabe-rare-sase-rareru** (*to be caused to be devoured*). This, I am afraid, is pushing our way too far beyond the scope of elementary Japanese. But I am simply showing the convenience of an agglutinative language which can express most intricate ideas by simple stringing of suffixes.

Also, it may be mentioned in passing that in Japanese it is quite usual to make passive of an intransitive verbs, as **Watakushi-wa sono hito-ni ik-are-te-shimai-mashita** (*I was walked out on—He walked out on me*).

Vocabulary :

" toranku "	*trunk,* also *suitcase*
" suteeshon "	*railway station*
kisha	*train*

Exercises :

Watakushi-wa kodomo-ni o-kashi-wo tabe-sase-mashita.	I let the child eat some cakes.
Watakushi - wa kodomo - ni gakkoo-no hon-wo ka-wase-mashita.	I let the child buy some school books.
Kono toranku-wo otoko-ni motte-ik-ase-mashoo ka?	Shall I have the man take this trunk over ?
Hai, kore-wo suteeshon-ni motte-ik-ase-te-kudasai.	Yes, please have this carried to the station.
Kisha-no kippu-wo ka-wase-mashoo.	Let us have the train ticket bought.
Kono hako-wo watakushi-ni motte-ik-ase-te-kudasai.	Please let me carry this box.
Hai, kore-wo mot-ase-te-age-mashoo.	Yes, I will let you carry this.
Suteeshon made aruite-ik-ase-te-kudasai.	Please let me walk to the station.
Keredomo kono kodomo-wo aruk-ase-nai-de-kudasai.	But please do not let this child walk.
Kono toranku-wa taisetsu-desu kara, hito-ni mot-ase-nai-de kudasai.	As this trunk is precious, please do not let any one (else) carry it.

Watakushi-wa densha-ni noru koto-ga deki-nakatta kara, uchi made aruk-ase-rare-mashita.

Because I could not get on the street car, I was forced to walk home.

LESSON 51

Regular Adjectives

Example:

Kore-wa yoi.   *This is good.*

The above sentence has no verb in it, and we see that a Japanese sentence can be formed without a verb, and that a regular adjective can act as a predicate. This is a blunt expression somewhat in the nature of the use of verbs without **masu,** and it is generally used in subordinate clause only, as **Kore-wa yoi to omoi-masu** (*I think this is good*).

A regular adjective has an inflexion much like that of a verb:

Adjective Stem	Ending	Words that Follow
	ku	nai nakatta nakaroo naku ari-masu etc.
yo		
	ku	aru atta aroo

$$\left\{ \begin{array}{l} \text{are (Command)} \\ \text{a} \text{ri-masu} \\ \quad \textbf{and all verbs} \end{array} \right.$$

i
$$\left\{ \begin{array}{l} \text{hito} \\ \text{toki} \\ \textit{and all nouns. Also} \\ \textit{this ending can be used} \\ \textit{at the end of a sentence.} \end{array} \right.$$

kere   ba (Conditional)

Command, or Imperative, is lacking in the inflexion of adjectives. It is taken care of by the use of the verb **aru** after the **ku** ending—**yoku are** (*be good*).

There is no irregular inflexion among the Japanese adjectives.

Now, let us examine the use of adjectives according to their inflexions:

Kore-wa yoku-nai.
> *This is not good.*

Kore-wa yoku ari-masu.
> *This is good.*

Kono hito-wa yoku aruki-masu.
> *He walks well.*

Kore-wa yoi hito-de su.
> *This is a good man.*

Kore-wa yoi.
> *This is good.*

Kore-ga yokereba, age-mashoo.
If this is good, I will give it to you.

As seen in the above examples, an adjective with **ku** ending acts as an adverd. There is no real distinction between adjectives and adverbs—when employed with **i** ending to modify a noun, it is an adjective, when employed with **ku** ending to modify a verb, or another adjective, it is an adverb. The ending **kere** is Conditional when followed by **ba**. There are other words to follow this ending, but their use is rare, and is not given in this lesson.

As for noun-adjectives, naturally there is no inflexion. When used as adjectives, they take **-na** or **-no** and when used as adverds they take **-ni** or no ending at all:—

shinsetsu-na hito	*a kind man* (adjective use)
shinsetsu-ni hanasu	*to speak kindly* (adverbial use)
sukoshi-no pan	*a little bread* (adjective use)
sukoshi taberu	*to eat a little* (adverbial use)

Vocabulary:

tooi	*far* (regular adjective)
chikai	*near* (regular adjective)
omoshiroi	*interesting* (regular adjective)
hanashi	*a story*
hanasu	*to tell* (verb of Group I)
ko	*child* (short for **kodomo**)

Exercises :

Kore-ga ichi-ban yoi to omoi-masu ka?	Do you think this is best?
Iie, sore-wa ichi-ban yoi to omoi-masen.	No, I do not think that is best.
Iie, sore-wa yoku-nai to omoi-masu.	No, I think that is not good.
Sore yori kore-ga yoi to omoi-masu.	I think this is better than that.
Kono mittsu-no hako-no na-ka-de dore-ga ichi-ban chii-sai to omoi-masu ka?	Among these three boxes which do you think is the smallest?
Watakushi-wa kore-ga ichi-ban chiisai to omoi-masu.	I think this is the smallest.
Kono ko-wa yoku aruk-are-masu.	This child can walk well.
Kono ko-wa yoku aruku ko to-ga deki-masu.	This child can walk well.
Kono hito-wa watakushi yo-ri hayaku aruku koto-ga deki-masu.	This person can walk faster than I.
Suteeshon-wa tooku ari-masu ka, chikaku ari-masu ka?	Is the station far or near?
Suteeshon-ga tookereba, den sha-de iki-mashoo.	If the station is far, let us go by the street car.
Suteeshon-ga chikakereba aruite-iki-mashoo.	If the station is near, let us go on foot.
Suteeshon-wa tooku nakaroo to omoi-masu kara aruite iki-mashoo.	I think the station is not far, so let us go on foot.
Anata-wa kono hon-ga omo shiroi to omoi-masu ka?	Do you think this book is interesting?

Hai, kore-wa anata-ni omoshi-roku-aroo to omoi-masu.

Yes, I think this will be interesting to you.

Kore-ga omoshirokereba yon-de-mi-yoo to omoi-masu.

If this is interesting, I think I will read it.

Sono sensei-wa shinsetsu-na hito-de su.

That teacher is a kind man.

Sono sensei-wa watakushi-ni Ei-go-wo shinsetsu-ni oshie-mashita.

That teacher taught me English kindly.

Koko-ni takusan-no okashi-ga ari-masu.

Here are a great deal of cakes.

Sore-wo takusan tabe-ma-shoo.

Let us eat them a great deal.

Kore-wo kirei-na kami-ni ki-rei-ni kaite-kudasai.

Please write this nicely on a clean sheet of paper.

LESSON 52

I like ; I want

Tōkyō-no Machi

Examples :

Watakushi-wa hon-ga hoshii (hoshiku ari-masu.)

I want a book.

Watakushi-wa hon-ga yomi-tai (yomi-taku ari-masu).

I want to read a book.

Watakushi-wa hon-ga suki-de su.

I am fond of a book.

Watakushi-wa hon-wo yomu koto-ga suki-de su.

I am fond of reading a book.

Key Words:

hoshii	*desirous of (to want)* ; used after a noun
-tai	*desirous of (to want to)* ; used after a verb
suki	*fond of* (noun-adjective)

Hoshii is a regular adjective and inflects as such—**hoshiku, hoshii, hoshikere.** **-Tai** is an auxiliary verb, but its inflexion is that of an adjective—**-taku, -tai, -takere.** **Suki** is a noun-adjective.

Note that in the above examples, **-wa** and **-ga** are used in one sentence together. In Lesson 47 it was mentioned that **-wa** and **-ga** are often used as endings of emphasis. Here is a good example, for in the first of the above sentences, **hon** is the most important word and it should be emphasised above all other words though, according to the logic of European grammar, it is merely an object. If an emphasis is wanted on **Watakushi,** implying " I am the one who wants, etc.," **-ga** may be given to it and **-wo** to **hon.** Or **-ga** may be given to both of them.

Vocabulary:

machi	*street, town*
" birujingu "	*building*
kazoeru	*to count* (verb of Group II)

jimusho	*office*
jidoosha	*motor car*
jitensha	*bicycle*
kai	*floor* (as *second floor*)

Exercises :

Anata-wa Yokohama-ni iki-tai to omoi-masu ka? — Do you think you want to go to Yokohama ?

Iie, watakushi-wa Yokohama-ni iki-taku ari-masen. — No, I don't want to go to Yokohama.

Watakushi-wa Tōkyō-ni itte-mi-tai to omoi-masu. — I think I want to go and see Tōkyō.

Koko-ni anata-no suki-na Tō-kyō-no e-ga ari-masu. — Here is a picture of your favourite Tōkyō.

Ookii birujingu-no mae-ni hi-to-ga hitori aruite-i-masu. — In front of a big building, there is a man walking.

Kono birujingu-ni mado-ga ikutsu ari-masu ka, anata-ni kazoe-rare-masu ka? — How many windows there are to this building, can you count?

Kono e-ni jidoosha-ga ikutsu aru ka, anata-ni kazoe-rare-masu ka? — How many motor cars there are in this picture, can you count?

Watakushi-no jimusho-wa ha-chi-kai-ni ari-masu. — My office is on the eighth floor.

Watakushi-wa sono jimusho-ga taihen suki-de su. — I like that office very much.

Watakushi-wa sono jimusho-ni iku koto-ga taihen suki-de su. — I like to go to that office very much.

Kono e-no migi-ni aru jidoo-sha-wa watakushi-no-de su. — The motor car at the right of this picture is mine.

Anata-wa jidoosha-ga hoshi-ku ari-masen ka?	Don't you want a motor car?
Anata-wa jidoosha-ni nori-ta-ku ari-masen ka?	Don't you want to ride in a car?
Anata-ga ima nori-takereba, nor-ase-te-age-mashoo.	If you wish to take a ride now, I will let you.
Anata-ga jitensha-ga hoshike-reba, ima katte-age-mashoo.	If you want a bicycle, I will buy it for you now.
Kodomo-ni okashi-ga tabe-sa-se-takereba, watakushi-no uchi-ni ko-sase-te kudasai.	If you wish to let children eat some cakes, let them come to my house.
Watakushi-wa hito-ni Tōkyō-no ookii machi-wo mi-sase-tai toki-ni, sono hito-wo ji-musho-ni ko-sase-masu.	When I wish to show people the big streets of Tōkyō, I let them come to my office.
Watakushi-no jimusho kara machi-ga yoku mi-rare-ma-su.	From my office one can see the streets well.

LESSON 53

If and Must

Examples (**1**):

Moshimo anata-ga kore-wo yomu naraba, yoi koto-wo oboe-mashoo.

If you read this, you will learn something good.

Moshimo anata-ga kore-wo yoma-nai naraba, yoi koto-wo oboe-nai-de shoo.

If you do not read this, you will not learn a good thing.

The idea of **if** is expressed by the combination of **moshimo** and **naraba**. The above examples show the full and proper form, but **moshimo** may be left out without impairing the meaning :—

Anata-ga kore-wo yomu naraba, yoi koto-wo obo-e-mashoo. (and negative)
> *If you read this, you will learn something good.* (and negative)

The presence of **moshimo** makes the sentence more emphatic.

There are several other sets of words to express conditional in Japanese, but here is given only one of them which has the widest applications. **Naraba** may be used in a sentence in which an adjective acts as predicate :—

Moshimo kono hon-ga omoshiroi naraba, yomi-mashoo.
> *If this book is interesting, I will read it.*

The same idea can be expressed with practically no change in its shade of meaning by the use of conditional ending of the adjective itself :—

Moshimo kono hon-ga omoshirokereba, yomi-mashoo,
> *If this book is interesting, I will read it.*

In many languages the Conditional employs past tense in expressing improbable or impossible ideas. One would say in English, "If I were a bird, etc." In Japanese the past tense is employed quite in the same way :—

"**Moshimo watakushi-ga tori-de atta naraba,** etc."

The elementary instruction in the Japanese language designed for thirty hours should end about here. The subtle uses of Conditional is more in the nature of advanced studies, but an introduction to it has been included here for two reasons. Firstly to satisfy the curiosity of some students who look further forward than is required for the moment, and secondly because it leads up to the most important application of the Conditional in expressing the Obligation—*must.*

Example (2):

Anata-wa sore-wo mi-nakereba nari-masen.
   You must see it.
Anata-wa sore-wo mi-tewa nari-masen.
   You must not see it.

Key Words :

moshimo—naraba	*if*
moshimo —kereba	*if*
-nakereba nara-nai (nari-masen)	*must*
-tewa nara-nai (nari-masen)	*must not*

-Nakereba is the conditional form of **nai.** Although

nai is an auxiliary verb (and also a verb, the negative of **aru**), it has an inflexion of a regular adjective—**naku, nai, nakere.**

The original meaning of the verb, **naru** of **nari-ma-sen** (**nara-nai**) is *to become.* In the above usage it means perhaps *nothing good will become of it.* And so a literal translation of the first sentence may be *If you don't see it, nothing good will come of it* or *that won't do—You must see it.*

Since *must* is expressed by the negative form **-nake-.eba**, *must not* is expressed by the affirmative form **-tewa** which may be regarded as combination of the connective **-te** and the ending **-wa** which is often used after a subject implying *in the case of.* And so, it is easy to see that **-tewa** can mean *if.* The second of the above examples may be translated literally as *If you see it, that won't do—You must not see it.*

The Japanese language has no single word to correspond to *must*, and the only way to express the idea is by this round-about conditional sentence. However, to a Japanese who employs this expression constantly **-nakereba nari-masen** is no more than one word of eight syllables.

Vocabulary :

nochi-ni	*later on*
hoka-no	*other, some other*

Exercises :

Watakushi-wa ashita gakkoo-ni ika-nakereba nari-masen.   I must go to school tomorrow.

Anata-wa ashita gakkoo-ni ittewa nari-masen.	You must not go to school tomorrow.
Anata-wa kore-wo kirei-ni ka-ka-nakereba nari-masen.	You must write this nicely.
Watakushi-wa kinoo kono hon-wo yonde-shimawa-na-kereba nari-masen deshita.	I had to finish reading this book yesterday.
Kono ko-ga komari-masu ka-ra, anata-wa hayaku aruite-wa nari-masen.	Because this child has difficulty (walking fast), you must not walk so fast.
Anata-ga ashita kuru naraba, yoi mono-wo age-mashoo.	If you would come to-morrow, I will give you something nice.
Ima Nippon-go-wo oboe-na-kereba, anata-wa nochi-ni komari-mashoo.	If you do not learn Japa-nese now, you will be troubled later on.
Moshimo anata-ni iku koto-ga deki-nakereba, watakushi-ga iki-mashoo.	If you cannot go, I will go.
Moshimo anata-ni Nippon-go-ga deki-nakereba, kono ji-musho-ni iru koto-wa deki-masen.	If you cannot speak Japa-nese, you cannot be in this office.
Anata-ga kono jimusho-ga suki-de nakereba, hoka-no jimusho-ni itte-kudasai.	If you are not fond of this office, please go to some other office.
Motto hayaku aruk-are-nake-reba, anata-wa kisha-ni nor-are-masen deshoo.	If you cannot walk faster, you will not be able to board the train.
Gohan-ga nakereba, anata-wa pan-wo tabe-nakereba nari-masen deshoo.	If there is no rice, you will have to eat some bread.

LESSON 54

Review Lesson

Lafcadio Hearn-no Uchi

Vocabulary :

sumu (sunda = sumi-ta)	*to live, to reside* (verb of Group I)
naru	*to become* (Group I)
namae	*name*
oku-san	*wife, mistress of the house*
tame-ni	*in order that*
nagai	*long* (regular adjective)
Chuu-gakkoo	*Middle School*

ishi-dooroo	stone lantern
kabe	wall
kinen	memorial
Teikoku Daigaku	Imperial University
shinu	to die (Group I)

Exercises :

Lafcadio Hearn-wa Nippon-no koto-wo takusan kaita hito-de su.

Lafcadio Hearn is the man who wrote a great deal about things Japanese.

Hearn-wa Nippon-ga taihen suki-de shita kara nochi-ni Nippon-no hito-ni nari-mashita ;

Hearn was fond of Japan very much, and so later he became a Japanese ;

Soshite Nippon-no namae-wo tsukuri-mashita.

And he made up a Japanese name.

Lafcadio Hearn-no Nippon-no namae-wa Koizumi Yagumo to ii-masu.

Lafcadio Hearn's Japanese name is Koizumi Yagumo.

Koizumi-wa oku-san-no namae-de su.

Koizumi is his wife's name.

Oku-san-wa Nippon-no hito-de shita.

His wife was Japanese.

Hearn-wa Nippon-no koto-wo kaku tame-ni Sen Happyaku Kyuu-juu Nen-ni Amerika kara ki-mashita.

In 1890 Hearn came from America in order to write about things Japanese.

Hearn-wa Nippon-ga suki-ni nari-mashita kara, Nippon-ni nagaku iru tame-ni gakkoo-no sensei-ni nari-mashita.

Hearn became fond of Japan, and so in order to stay in Japan long he became a teacher in a school.

Sono gakkoo-wa Matsue-no Chuu-gakkoo-de shita.	That school was a Middle School in Matsue.
Sono toshi-no Juu-ni Gatsu-ni Koizumi Setsuko-ga oku-san-ni nari mashita.	In December of that year Miss Setsuko Koizumi became his wife.
Kore-wa sono toki Hearn to oku-san-ga sunda uchi-no e-de su.	This is the picture of the house in which Hearn and his wife lived at that time.
Kore-wa chiisai uchi-de su, keredomo yoi uchi-de su.	This is a small house, but it is a good house.
Niwa-no ki-no shita-ni ishi-dooroo-ga ari-masu.	Under the tree in the garden there is a stone lantern.
Hidari-no kabe-no mae-ni aru ikebana-ga mi-rare-masu ka?	Can you see the flower arrangement in front of the wall on the left?
Kono uchi-wa Matsue-ni ari-masu.	This house is in Matsue.
Machi-no hito-wa kono uchi-wo Yagumo-no kinen-no uchi to ii-masu.	The town people call this house the memorial house of Yagumo.
Hearn-no oku-san-wa Nippon-no hanashi-wo takusan shi-mashita.	Mrs. Hearn told many Japanese stories.
Soshite Hearn-wa sore-wo Ei-go-de kaki-mashita.	And Hearn wrote them in English.
Futari-ga kono uchi-ni sunde-i-ta toki-ni, takusan-no hon-ga kak-are-mashita.	When the two were living in this house, many books were written.

Nochi-ni Hearn-wa Tōkyō-no Teikoku Daigaku-no sensei-ni nari-mashita;

Later on Hearn became a teacher in the Imperial University of Tokyo.

Soshite Tōkyō-ni sumi-mashita.

And he lived in Tokyo.

Hearn-wa yoi sensei-de shita, soshite rippa-na hito-de shita;

Hearn was a good teacher and he was a fine man:

Soshite hon-wo yoku kaki-mashita.

And he wrote books well.

Hearn-wa Sen Kyuu-hyaku Yo Nen-no Ku Gatsu Ni-juu-roku Nichi-ni shini-mashita.

Hearn died on September 26th, 1904.

Sono toki Hearn-wa go-juu-go-de shita.

At that time Hearn was fifty-five.

Soshite san-nin-no otoko-no ko to hitori-no onna-no ko-ga ari-mashita.

And there were (he had) three sons and a daughter.

Hearn-wa shinu made Nippon no koto-wo kaite-i-mashita.

Hearn was writing about Japan until he died.

Moshimo sono toki-ni shina-nakatta naraba, motto taku-san-no hon-wo kaita-de shoo.

If he did not die at that time, he would have written more books.

APPENDICES

APPENDICES

Japanese Writing and Pronunciation

In writing, a Japanese employs Chinese characters and kana together. A Chinese character has its individual meaning as well as the sounds, and it is employed for nouns, verbs, adjectives and such "solid" words. A kana represents merely a syllabic sound and it has no meaning of its own. It is employed for endings, postpositions and such parts of less import. There are forty-eight letters in kana while there are a limitless number of Chinese characters. A Japanese typewriter has some 2300 types on its type board and several hundred more in reserve. Chinese characters certainly make a great obstacle in the way of studying the written Japanese.

It is not impossible to write everything in kana, but that will betray the lack of education on the part of the writer. Indeed, the original meaning of the word **kana** is *substitute letter*, and the Chinese characters are considered *real letters* (**hon-ji**). Although the Chinese characters are difficult to learn, once they are learned and mastered, they make a most rapid reading possible, because they convey the meaning directly to the eyes without resorting to the "sound."

In this book, which is designed for an elementary instruction in spoken Japanese, only an introduction to kana will be given and the Chinese characters will not be touched upon.

It is considered that there are fifty basic sounds in the Japanese language, and each of those sounds is represented by a kana. A table of those basic sounds and kana, generally called Aiueo Table, is given on the following page (Table I). There are some repetitions of sounds and kana because of the irregularity in the Japanese pronunciation, and in fact there are only forty-eight kana. Also, there are two pairs of kana—ｲ (i) and ヰ (i) of the second tier, and ェ (e) and (ヱ) (e) of the fourth tier—which have the same sounds. In olden times their sounds were distinct, but they have been broken down in the course of time. The one extra sound n (ン) is not counted in the table, because it does not constitute a syllable.

Note that there are two systems of kana. Those angular ones printed next to Romaji are called **kata kana** (stiff, formal kana) and those in curved lines printed below them are called **hira kana** (informal kana). The latter is in general use while the use of the former is somewhat in the nature of the italics in English. Also, in writing a very formal, official note kata kana is employed entirely.

These basic sounds are also called the *clear sounds* in contrast to those in Table II which are the *turbid sounds* (**nigori**). For instance, **ga gi gu ge go** are the turbid sound of **ka ki ku ke ko** and the turbidity is indicated by a sign of two dots on the upper right side of the kana. **pa pi pu pe po** are called the *half turbid sounds* of **ha hi fu he ho** and are marked by a circle to each of the kana.

Table IV shows the compound sounds. **Kya** is supposed to be a composite of **ki** and **ya,** and **ya** is written in small letter to indicate that it is to be read as a compound sound. Table V contains the compound sounds made turbid.

Counting off the duplication caused by the irregularity in the Japanese pronunciation, one may see that there are 106 distinct sounds in the language. The method of writing every one of them in kana is indicated in the table. When Romaji is employed, there is no need of distinguishing between the basic sounds and the compound or turbid sounds.

TABLE I

Fifty Basic Sounds

Aiueo

a	ka	sa	ta	na	ha	ma	ya	ra	wa	n
ア	カ	サ	タ	ナ	ハ	マ	ヤ	ラ	ワ	ン
あ	か	さ	た	な	は	ま	や	ら	わ	ん
i	ki	shi (si)	chi (ti)	ni	hi	mi	i	ri	i	
イ	キ	シ	チ	ニ	ヒ	ミ	イ	リ	ヰ	
い	き	し	ち	に	ひ	み	い	り	ゐ	
u	ku	su	tsu (tu)	nu	fu (hu)	mu	yu	ru	u	
ウ	ク	ス	ツ	ヌ	フ	ム	ユ	ル	ウ	
う	く	す	つ	ぬ	ふ	む	ゆ	る	う	
e	ke	se	te	ne	he	me	e	re	e	
エ	ケ	セ	テ	ネ	ヘ	メ	エ	レ	ヱ	
え	け	せ	て	ね	へ	め	え	れ	ゑ	
o	ko	so	to	no	ho	mo	yo	ro	wo	
オ	コ	ソ	ト	ノ	ホ	モ	ヨ	ロ	ヲ	
お	こ	そ	と	の	ほ	も	よ	ろ	を	

TABLE II
Turbid sounds

TABLE III
Half Turbid sounds

ga ガ が	za ザ ざ	da ダ だ	ba バ ば		pa パ ぱ
gi ギ ぎ	ji (di) ジ じ	ji (di) ヂ ぢ	bi ビ び		pi ピ ぴ
gu グ ぐ	zu ズ ず	zu ヅ づ	bu ブ ぶ		pu プ ぷ
ge ゲ げ	ze ゼ ぜ	de デ で	be ベ べ		pe ペ ぺ
go ゴ ご	zo ゾ ぞ	do ド ど	bo ボ ぼ		po ポ ぽ

Note: The Romaji employed in this book is of Hepburn System, but in these tables the Japanese System also is given in parenthesis whenever its spellings differ from those of Hepburn System. The Japanese System is an attempt to make the spelling appear simpler and more logical to the Japanese people.

TABLE IV
Compound sound

kya キャ きゃ	sha (sya) シャ しゃ	cha (tya) チャ ちゃ	nya ニャ にゃ	hya ヒャ ひゃ	mya ミャ みゃ	rya リャ りゃ
ki キ き	shi (si) シ し	chi (ti) チ ち	ni ニ に	hi ヒ ひ	mi ミ み	ri リ り
kyu キュ きゅ	shu (syu) シュ しゅ	chu (tyu) チュ ちゅ	nyu ニュ にゅ	hyu ヒュ ひゅ	myu ミュ みゅ	ryu リュ りゅ
ke ケ け	she (sye) シェ しぇ	che (tye) チェ ちぇ	ne ネ ね	hye ヒェ ひぇ	me メ め	re レ れ
kyo キョ きょ	sho (syo) ショ しょ	cho (tyo) チョ ちょ	nyo ニョ にょ	hyo ヒョ ひょ	myo ミョ みょ	ryo リョ りょ

Table V

Turbid Compound Sounds

Table VI

Half Turbid Compound Sounds

gya	ja (zya)		bya	pya
ギャ	ヂャ ジャ		ビャ	ピャ
ぎゃ	ぢゃ じゃ		びゃ	ぴゃ
gi	ji (di)		bi	pi
ギ	ヂ ジ		ビ	ピ
ぎ	ぢ じ		び	ぴ
gyu	ju (zyu)		byu	pyu
ギュ	ヂュ ジュ		ビュ	ピュ
ぎゅ	ぢゅ じゅ		びゅ	ぴゅ
ge	je (zye)		be	pe
ゲ	ヂェ ジェ		ベ	ペ
げ	ぢぇ じぇ		べ	ぺ
gyo	jo (zyo)		byo	pyo
ギョ	ヂョ ジョ		ビョ	ピョ
ぎょ	ぢょ じょ		びょ	ぴょ

Foreign Words In the Japanese Language

The following list of foreign words in the Japanese language was compiled as a class work by the first year boys of Keio Middle School (Keio Futsubu) who were just beginning to study English. Therefore it is safe to assume that all the words in the list are understood and employed by the Japanese who has no knowledge of English as a language. It is surprising to find how many English words the Japanese have adopted without being conscious of it.

In the following list the Japanese pronunciations which have been too far changed from the original are indicated in the parenthesis. They are mostly the words adopted in very early days.

accent
album
alcohol
all right (oorai)
aluminium (arumi *or* nyu-
    umu)
amateur
announcer
antenna
apartment (apaato)
apron
arc
arch

asparagus
asphalt
baby
back
bacteria
bakery
balance
balcony
ball
banana
band belt, brass band
bar drinking place
baseball

basket

basket ball

bat baseball bat

battery **electric**

bed

beefsteak (bifuteki)

beer (biiru)

bell

belt

bench

best

Bible

biscuit

black list

blanket (ketto)

boat

boat house

boat race

boiler

bonbon

bonus

book

bourgeois

boxer

boxing

boy

boycott

boy scout

brake

brandy

broker

brush

bucket (baketsu)

building

bus

butter

button (botan)

cabaret

cabbage (kyabetsu)

cable car

cafe

cake

calendar

camera

camera man

camouflage

camp

can (kan)

candy

canoe

captain

caramel

carbon paper

card

case **container**

catalogue

catarrh (kataru)

catch ball

cellophane

celluloid

cement

cigar

cigar lighter

cigarette case

chalk **crayon**

champion
chance
chandelier
change
cheese
cherry
chewing gum
chicken
chocolate
cholera
chorus
Christmas
Christmas tree
chrome
cider
cinema (kinema *or* shinema)
circus
class
classmate
cleaning **dry cleaning**
club **association**
coach **sports coach**
coal-tar
cocktail
cocoa
coffee (koohii)
coil
collar
comma
compass
concrete
condensed milk

condition
cook **a cheff**
copy
cork
corned beef
cosmos
count
course
court **as tennis court**
cream
croquette (korokke)
cuff (kafusu)
cup **sports trophy**
curtain
curve (kaabu)
cushion
cut **illustration**
cutlet (katsuretsu)
cylinder

dahlia
dam
dance
dancer
deck
delicate
demonstration
department store(depaato)
desk
diagram
diamond
Diesel
dock **dry dock**

doctor
dollar
door
double
double collar
dozen (daasu)
drive
dry cleaning
dry ice
dynamite

ebonite
elevator
enamel
encore
engine
episode
escalator

fan **as sports fan**
feet **unit of length**
film
flannel
foot **unit of length**
foot ball
fork
frock coat
fruit punch
fry
fry pan
full speed
fuse

gaiter (geetoru)
gallon
game
gang **gangster**
garage
gas (gasu)
gasoline
gauze (gaaze)
girl
glass (garasu)
glider
go **traffic signal**
goal
golf link
gorilla
gossip
gram
graph
grill **Restaurant**
ground **as base ball ground**
group
guide
guide book
guitar

hair net
hall **auditorium**
ham
hammer
hammock
handbag
handkerchief (hankachi)
handle

harmonica
head-light
heart **of card game**
helmet
hike
hiking
hint
hockey
home
home run
hook (hokku)
hose **water hose**
hot cake
hotel **foreign style hotel**
humour
hurdle
husband
hysteria (histerii)

ice
icecream
ice hockey
ice water
inch
inflation
influenza
ink
iron (airon) **flat iron**

jacket (jaketsu)
jam **food**
jazz
jelly

jump
kangaroo
khaki
kick
king
kiss
knife
knock
knock out
kodak

lace
lamp
lead **a verb**
leader
left
lemon
lens
linen
linoleum
lion
litre (rittoru)
lucky
lunch

macaroni
machine (mishin) **sewin**
    machine
magnesium
magnet
mamma
manage **a verb**
manager

manikin

mantle

marathon

march **music**

mark

market

mascot

mask

mast

mat

medal

megaphone

member

memo

mental test

meter (meetaa **or** meetoru)

metre (meetaa **or** meetoru)

microphone (maiku *or* mai kurohon)

mile

milk

minus

model

modern

monkey

morning coat

mosaic

motor

motor boat

motto

muslin (mosurin)

napkin

naphthalene

necktie

neon sign

net

new

news

nickel

nicotine

no

no count

nonsense

note

notebook

number

oblate (obraato)

office

oil

O. K.

omelet (omuretsu)

opera

orange

orchestra

organ **music**

overcoat (kooto *or* oobaa)

overshoes

ozone

page

pajama

pallet

pamphlet

panorama

pants

papa

paper

parachute

paraffin

parasol

pass

pedal

pen

percent

permanent wave

pet

pianist

piano

picnic

pin

pincette

pineapple

ping pong

pipe

pistol

piston

plan

platform **of railway station**

platinum (purachina)

play **a sports term**

pocket

pool **swimming pool**

pose

post **post box**

poster

potato

pound (pondo)

prism

program

proletariat

propeller

pulp

pump (ponpu)

putty (pate)

pyramid

race **sports**

racket **tennis**

radio (rajio)

radio drama (rajio dorama)

radium (rajuumu)

rail

raincoat

rayon

ready

ready-made

rear-car

record **highest record, phonograph record**

regular

relay

restaurant

review **theatrical**

rhythm

ribbon

rice

rice curry

right

rink **sports**

roast (roosu)

robbot

rocket

Roentgen

roller

roller skate

romance

romantic

rope

ruby

rucksack

Rugby

runner **sports**

running **sports**

rush hour

sabotage

safe **sports term**

sailor

salon

sample

sandwich

Santa Claus

sauce

sausage

scarf

score

score board

scrap

scrapbook

screen

screw **propeller**

search-light

season

seesaw

sensation

sensational

sentimental

service

set

shawl

sheet

shirt (shatsu) **under shirt**

shovel

shower **-bath**

show window

shutter

sidecar

sign

silk hat

siren

skate

sketch

sketch book

ski

skirt

slate

slipper

smart

socker **-game**

soda

sofa

soft hat

soprano

soup

speed

speed up

spike
sponge
sports
spring steel spring
spy
stage
stamp
staple fibre (su fu)
start
station railway station
steam -heating
stew
stock
stop
stopwatch
stove
straw tube
strawberry
strike
sweater
switch
symbol
syrup

table
table speech
talkie
tank reservoir, war machine
tape
taxi
team sports
television

tennis
tenor
tent
test
text (tekisuto)
thank you
tile
tip gratuity
tire rubber tire
toast
tobacco
toilet paper
tomato
ton
touch
tourist bureau
tournament
towel
tractor
truck
trump card game
trunk also suit case
tulip
tunnel (tonneru)
typewriter
typist

umpire
uniform
utopia

varnish (wanisu or nisu)
vaseline

veil

velvet

veneer (beniya)

violin

vitamin (bitamin)

wafers

waffle

Watt

whisky

white shirt (waishatsu) **also striped or coloured shirts**

wrestling

yacht **sail boat**

yard (yaado *or* yaaru) **unit of length**

yes

zero

Abbreviations

n.	noun
v. t.	transitive verb
v. i.	intransitive verb
I.	verb of Group I
II.	verb of Group II
irr.	irregular verb
adj.	regular adjective
n-adj.	noun-adjective
(adj.)	adjective use of other parts of speech
adv.	adverb
auxil. v.	auxiliary verb
postp.	postposition
suf.	suffix
pref.	prefix
con.	conjuction, connective
pron.	pronoun
interj	interjection

Numerals in parenthesis indicate the lessons in which the words are explained.

Japanese-English Vocabulary

A

abunai *adj*. dangerous

abura *n*. oil ; fat

agaru *v.i. I*. to go up

ageru *v.t. II*. to give ; to send up, to raise (27, 46)

ago *n*. jaw

ai *n*. love

ai-rashii *adj*. lovely, charming

ai-rashisa *n*. loveliness

aisatsu *n*. greeting

aisatsu-suru *v.i. irr*. to greet

ai-suru *v.t. irr*. to love

aji *n*. taste

aka *n*. red.   **akai** *adj*. red

akari *n*. light

akarui *adj*. light

akeru *v.t. II*. to open (17)

ake-te-iku to leave something open (24)

aki *n*. autumn

akiru *v.i. II*. to be tired of

aku *v.i. I*. to open

amai *adj*. sweet (in taste)

amari *n*. remainder

amaru *v.i. I*. to be left over

amasa *n*. sweetness (in taste)

ame *n*. rain

ami *n*. net

ana *n*. hole

anata *pron*. you (2)

ane *n*. elder sister

ani *n*. elder brother

annai *n*. guide, guidance

annai-suru *v.t. irr*. to guide

anzen *n*. safety. **anzen-na** *n-adj*. safe

ao *n*. blue.   **aoi** *adj*. blue

arai *adj*. rough

ar-areru can be, possible (47)

arasoi *n*. quarrel

arasou *v.i. I*. to quarrel, to contest

aratamaru *v.i. I*. to be revised

aratameru *v.t. II*. to revise

arau *v.t. I*. to wash

arawasu *v.t. I*. to show

are *pron*. that

-areru *auxil. v*. can ; passive voice (47, 49)

ari *n*. ant

arigatai *adj*. kind, fortunate

arigatoo thank you (27)

aru *v.i. irr*. to be (41)

aru (*adj*.) a certain

aruite-iku go on foot (24)

aruku *v.i. v.t. I*. to walk (24)

asa *n*. morning

asa *n*. hemp

asa-gohan *n*. breakfast (26)

asai *adj*. shallow

asa-sa *n*. shallowness ⌈(50)

-aseru *auxil. v*. to let (causative)

ashi *n.* foot, leg

ashita *n.* tomorrow (22, 36)

asobi *n.* play, game

asobu *v. i. I.* to play (42)

asonda played, past form of *asobu*

asonde-i-masu is playing (42)

ataeru *v.t. II.* to give

atai *n.* price, value ⌈worth

atai-suru *v.i. irr.* to cost, to be

atama *n.* head

atarashii *adj.* new

atarashi-sa *n.* newness

atatakai *adj.* warm

atataka-sa *n.* warmth

atsui *adj.* thick

atsui *adj.* hot

atsumari *n.* gathering, meeting

atsumaru *v.i. I.* to gather

atsumeru *v.t. II.* to gather

atsu-sa *n.* thickness

atsu-sa *n.* hotness, heat

atta was, were. past form of

au *v.i. I.* to meet ⌊aru (40)

awaseru *v.t. II.* to put together

ayamari *n.* mistake

ayamaru *v.t. I.* to mistake

ayamaru *v.i. I.* to apologize

ayamatta *(adj.)* mistaken

azukaru *v.t. I.* to take charge of

azukeru *v.t. II.* to deposit, to entrust

B

bai *suf.* times, fold (ni-bai twice as much)

baikin *n.* bacteria

baka *n. interj.* fool

bakari *suf.* about, only

baketsu *n.* bucket

bakuhatsu *n.* explosion

bakuhatsu-suru *v.i. irr.* to explode

ban *n.* evening

ban *suf.* number, -th (33)

bangoo *n.* number (33)

ban-suru *v.t. irr.* to stand guard

banme *suf.* number,-th (33)

bara *n.* rose

bassuru *v.t. irr.* to punish

batsu *n.* punishment

beki *auxil. v.* should, must

benjo *n.* water-closet

benkyoo *n.* study

benkyoo-suru *v.t. irr.* to study

benri *n.* convenience

benri-na *n-adj.* convenient

betsu-no *n-adj.* separate

biiru *n.* beer

bin *n.* bottle

binboo-na *n-adj.* poor, destitute

boku *pron.* I

bonyari-shita *(adj.)* vague

boo *n.* stick, pole

booshi *n.* hat, cap

botan *n.* button

budoo *n* grapes

buji *n.* safety. buji-ni *adv.* without mishap

bun *n.* sentence

bun *n.* portion

bunka *n.* culture, civilization

bunryoo *n.* quantity

burei-na *n-adj.* discourteous

buta *n.* pig

butai *n.* detachment

butai *n.* theater stage

butsuri-gaku *n.* physics

byoo *n.* second (unit of time) (35)

byoo *n.* tack, rivet

byoo-in *n.* hospital

byooki *n.* disease

byoo-nin *n.* sick person

C

cha *n.* tea (16)

chabu-dai *n.* dining table (26)

chawan *n.* rice-bowl (26)

chi *n.* blood

chichi *n.* father

chie *n.* intelligence

chigau (*adj.*) different, wrong

chiisai *adj.* small (5)

chijimeru *v.t. II.* to shorten

chijimu *v.i. I.* to shrink

chika *n-adj.* underground

chikai *adj.* near (51)

chikara *n.* strength

chika-shitsu *n.* basement

chika-tetsu *n.* subway

chikuonki *n.* phonograph

chirasu *v.t. I.* to scatter

chiri *n.* dust

chiri *n.* geography

chiru *v.i. I.* to fall, to scatter

chishiki *n.* knowledge

choo *numeral* 1,000,000,000,000

shoocho *n.* butterfly

choosetsu *n.* adjustment

choosetsu-suru *v.t. irr.* to adjust

chootsugai *n.* hinge

choowa *n.* harmony

choowa-suru *v.i. irr.* to harmonize

chuu-gakkoo *n.* middle school (54)

chuugi *n.* loyalty. chuugi-na *n-adj.* loyal

chuui *n.* attention, care

chuui-suru *v.t. irr.* to be watchful of

chuumon *n.* order

chuumon-suru *v.t. irr.* to order

chuuoo *n.* middle, center

D

dai *n.* subject

dai *pref.* number, -th

dai *n.* base, stool, table

dai *numeral adjunct* "unit," used for cars and machinery (31)

daigaku *n.* university (54)

daihyoo *n.* representative

daihyoo-suru *v.t. irr.* to represent

daiji-na *n-adj.* precious

daijoobu-na *n-adj.* safe, secure

dairi *n.* deputy, proxy

dairi-wo suru *v. i. irr.* to take someone's place

daku *v.t. I.* to hold, to enbrace

dakyoo *n.* compromise

damaru *v.i. I.* to grow silent, to

shut up

damasu *v.t. I.* to deceive

dame *n-adj. interj.* no good

dan *n.* step, tier (39)

dantai *n.* group, party

dare *pron.* who?

dasu *v.t. I.* to take out, to put out

-de ending for predicate comp-lement (1)

-de in, among, abbreviation of **no-naka-de** (34)

de *postp.* by means of, in, at (38)

dekiru *v.i. II.* to be able (48)

Denka *suf.* Prince, Princess

denki *n.* electricity (16)

denpoo *n.* telegram

densha *n.* electric car, street car (21)

denshin *n.* telegraph

dentoo *n.* electric light (16)

denwa *n.* telephone

deru *v.i. II.* to go out, to come out (24)

-de shita was, were (19)

-de shoo will be, shall be (22)

de-te-iku go out (24)

de-te-kuru come out (24)

do *suf.* time, as three times

do *suf.* degree

dobin *n.* tea kettle (of earthen ware) (26)

dochira *pron.* which?, where? which one (of the two)? (34)

doko *pron.* where? (9)

doku *n.* poison

domo *suf.* indicating plurality

donaru *v.i. I.* to yell

donata *pron.* who? (4)

donburi *n.* bowl

donna *n-adj.* what kind of? (5)

dono (*adj.*) which? (33)

doobutsu *n.* animal

doobutsu-en *n.* zoological gar-den

doogu *n.* tool, furniture

doojoo *n.* sympathy

dooro *n.* road

doozo *adv.* please, kindly (28)

dore *pron.* which?, which one (among many)? (8, 34)

doro *n.* soil, earth

doroboo *n.* theaf

Doyoobi *n.* Saturday (36)

E

e *n.* picture (39)

e *n.* handle

-e *postp.* to, toward

eda *n.* branch

eiga *n.* cinema, movie

Ei-go *n.* English language (38)

eikyoo *n.* influence, effect

eikyoo-suru *v.i. irr.* to influence

eki *n.* liquid, solution

eki *n.* railway station

en, yen unit of money

enpitsu *n.* pencil (8)

enryo *n.* reserve, modesty

enryo-suru *v.i. v.t. irr.* to be re-served

entotsu *n.* smokestack

erabu *v.t. I.* choose

F

fuda *n.* card, ticket, tag
fude *n.* writing brush
fuhei *n.* complaint
fujin *n.* lady, wife, Mrs.
fukai *adj.* deep
fukasa *n.* depth
fuku *v.t. I.* to blow
fuku *v.t. I.* to wipe
fukumu *v.t. I.* to imply
fukuramu *v.i. I.* to swell up
fukuro *n.* bag
fumu *v.t. I.* to step on, to trample
fun *n.* minute (unit of time) (35)
fune *n.* ship, boat
fureru *v.i. II.* to touch
fureru *v.i. II.* to swing, to shake
furo *n.* bath
furu *v.i. I.* to rain, to fall
furu *v.t. I.* to swing, to shake
furueru *v.i. II.* to tremble
furui *adj.* old, antiquated
fusagu *v.t. I.* to stop, to clog up
fusegu *v.t. I.* to defend
fusuma *n.* (heavy) paper door
futa *n.* cover, lid (4)
futa-kumi two sets (32)
futari two persons (32)
futatsu *numeral* two (28)
futoi *adj.* thick, big
futoru *v.i. I.* to grow fat
futotta *(adj.)* fat
futsuka two days, second day

of the month (36)
futsuu, futsuu-no *-adj.* ordinary
fuuzoku *n.* custom, manners
fuyu *n.* winter
fuzoku-suru *v.i. irr.* to belong

G

-ga ending for subject (emphatic) (8)
gai *n.* damage
gaikoku *n.* foreign country
gaikoo *n.* diplomacy
gai-suru *v.t. irr.* to damage
gaitoo *n.* overcoat
gakkoo *n.* school (14)
gakumon *n.* learning
ganjitsu New Year's Day (36)
gan-nen first year (of an era) (36)
garasu *n.* glass
gasu *n.* gas
gatsu *suf.* month
geijutsu *n.* fine arts
geki *n.* drama
gen-in *n.* cause
genkan *n.* entrance hall (39)
genki *n.* spirit, energy
genkin *n.* cash
genzuru *v.i. v.t. irr.* (inflexion of suru) to decrease
gesui *n.* sewerage
geta *n.* wooden clogs (39)
Getsuyoobi *n.* Monday (36)
gezai *n.* laxative
gimu *n.* duty

gin *n.* silver

ginkoo *n.* bank

giri *n.* obligation

go *numeral* five (30)

go *n.* language, word

go- *pref.* honorific

go-chisoo *n.* feast, entertainment

Go-gatsu month of May (36)

gogo *n.* afternoon

go-han *n.* boiled rice, meal (22)

gomen-nasai please forgive me

gozai-masu to be (ari-masu)

gozen *n.* before-noon, morning

guntai *n.* army

guuzen *n.* & *n-adj.* accidental (guuzen-no)

gyoo *n.* line of a page

H

ha *n.* leaf

ha *n.* tooth

ha *n.* edge (of a knife)

habuku *v.t. I.* to eliminate

hachi *n.* bee

hachi *numeral* eight (30)

Hachi-gatsu August (36)

hadaka-no *n-adj.* nude

hade-na *n-adj.* gay

hae (hai) *n.* fly

hagaki *n.* postcard

haha *n.* mother

hai *n.* lung; ashes

hai (hae) *n.* fly

hai yes (2)

hai *suf.* —ful, as cupful (31)

hairu *v.i. v.t. I.* to enter (39)

haita put on (past form of haku) (39)

haitta entered (past form of hairu) (39)

haji *n.* shame

haji-wo kaku to be disgraced

hajimaru *v.i. I.* to begin (42)

hajime *n.* beginning

hajimeru *v.t. II.* to begin

haka *n.* grave

hakama *n.* skirt, hakama

hakari *n.* measure, scale

hakaru *v.t. I.* to measure, to weigh

hake *n.* brush

hakken *n.* discovery

hakken-suru *v.t. irr.* to discover

hakkiri *adv.* distinctly, clearly

hakkiri-shita (*adj.*) distinct, clear

hakkiri-suru *v.i. irr.* to be or to become distinct

hako *n.* box (4)

haku *v.t. I.* to wear on foot (39)

haku *v.t. I.* to vomit

haku *v.t. I.* to sweep

hakubutsu-kan *n.* museum

han *n.* half, half past (35)

hana *n.* nose

hana *n.* flower

hanareru *v.i. II.* to part, to be distant

hanare-ta (*adj.*) separated, distant

hanashi *n.* story, talk (42, 51)

hanasu *v.t. I.* to separate

hanbun *n. & n-adj.* half (hanbun-no)

hane *n.* feather, wing

haneru *v.i. II.* to jump

hantai *n. n-adj.* opposition, opposite (hantai-no)

hantai-suru *v.i. irr.* to oppose

haori *n.* over-garment

hara *n.* stomach, abdomen

harau *v.t. I.* to pay, to sweep off

hare *n.* fine weather

hareru *v.i. II.* to clear up

hari *n.* needle

haru *n.* spring (season)

hasami *n.* scissors

hashi *n.* bridge

hashi *n.* end, margin

hashi (or o-hashi) *n.* chop sticks (26)

hashigo *n.* ladder

hashira *n.* pillar

hashiru *v.i. I.* to run

hata *n.* flag

hatake *n.* farm field

hataraki *n.* work

hataraku *v.i. I.* to work

hatsuka twenty days, twentieth day of the month (36)

hatsumei *n.* invention

hatsumei-suru *v.t. irr.* to invent

hayai *adj.* quick, early

haya-sa *n.* speed, earliness

hebi *n.* snake

Heika *suf., n.* his (her) Majesty

heikin *n.* average, balance

heikin-suru *v.t. irr.* to average, to balance

heikoo *n-adj.* parallel (heikoo-no)

heikoo-suru *v.i. irr.* to parallel

heitai *n.* soldiers

heiwa *n.* peace. **heiwa-na** *n-adj.* peaceful

henka *n.* change

henka-suru *v.i. irr.* to change, to transform

heri *n.* edge, brim

heta-na *n-adj.* unskilful, clumsy

heya *n.* room (7)

hi *n.* sun, sunshine, day (36)

hi *n.* fire

hibachi *n.* fire brazier (15)

hidari *n. & n-adj.* left (12)

hieru *v.i. II.* to become cool

higashi *n.* east

hijoo *n.* emergency

hijoo-ni *adv.* very, greatly

hikaku *n.* comparison

hikaku-suru *v.t. irr.* to compare

hikari *n.* light

hikaru *v.i. I.* to shine

hiki *numeral adjunct* "head," used for living things in general (31)

hikidashi *n.* drawer (33)

hikooki *n.* aeroplane

hiku *v.t. I.* to pull, to draw

hikui *adj.* low (34)

hima *n.* leisure, time

himitsu *n.* secret. **himitsu-no** *n-adj.* secret

himitsu-ni suru to keep secret

himo *n.* string, rope

hiraita (*adj.*) open

hiraki *n*, opening, door

hiraku *v.t. v.i. I.* to open

hiroi *adj.* wide (7)

hiro-sa *n.* width, area

hiru *n.* day-time, noon

hito *n.* person, man, woman (10)

hito-kumi one set (32)

hitori one person (32)

hitotsu *numeral* one (27)

hitotsu-mo (not) one, (not) any

hitsuyoo *n.* necessity. **hitsuyoo-na** *n-adj.* necessary

hiyasu *v.t. I.* to cool

hiza *n.* knee

ho *n.* sail

hodo *postp.* as, like, about

hodoku *v.t. I.* to untie

hogaraka-na *n-adj.* serene

hoka, hoka-no *n-adj.* other, some other (53)

hoken *n.* insurance

homeru *v.t. II.* to praise

hon *n.* book (1)

hon *numeral adjunct* "stick," used for long objects as pencils (31)

honbako *n.* bookcase (11)

hone *n.* bone

honoo *n.* flame

honyaku *n.* translation

honyaku-suru *v.t. irr.* to translate

hooritsu *n.* law

horu *v.t. I* to dig

hori *n.* moat

hoshi *n.* star

hoshii *adj.* desirous of, (to want) (52)

hotoke-sama *n.* Buddha

hotondo *adv.* almost

hyaku *numeral* hundred (30)

hyoo *n.* list, table

hyoojun *n.* standard

I

i *n.* stomach

ichi *n.* position

ichi *numeral* one (30)

Ichi-gatsu January (36)

ichigo *n.* strawberry

ido *n.* well

ie *n.* house

ii, yoi *adj.* good

iie no (3)

ijutsu *n.* medical art

ikani *adv.* however, how, how much

ikari *n.* anger ; anchor

ikaru *v.i. I.* to be angry

ikebana *n.* flower arrangement (26)

iki *n.* breath

iki-mono *n.* living thing

ikiru *v.i. II.* to live, to be alive

iki-te-iru (*adj.*) alive, living

iki-wo suru to breathe

iku, *pref.,* **ikutsu** *adv.* how many (29)

iku *v.i. I.* to go (20)

ikura *adv.* how much? (35)

ima *n. & adv.* now

imi *n.* meaning

imi-suru *v.t. irr.* to mean

imo *n.* potato

imooto *n.* younger sister

inaka *n.* countryside

inoru *v.t. I.* to pray

insatsu *n.* printing

insatsu-suru *v.t. irr.* to print

inu *n.* dog

ippai one (cup)-ful (32)

ippiki one " head " (32)

ippon one "stick "

ippun one minute (35)

iro *n.* colour

ireru *v.t. II.* to put in

iri-guchi *n.* entrance

iru *v.i. II.* to be (10)

iru *v.i. I.* to need (27)

isha *n.* physician

ishi *n.* stone (39)

ishi *n.* will, will power

ishi-dooro *n.* stone lantern (54)

ishiki *n.* consciousness

ishiki-suru *v.t. irr.* to be conscious

isogashii *adj.* busy

isogu *v.t. I.* to hurry

issatsu one volume (32)

issen one sen (35)

issho-ni *postp.* together

isu *n.* chair (34)

ita *n.* board

itadaki *n.* summit

itadaku *v.t. I.* to receive

itai *adj.* painful, sore

itameru *v.t. II.* to injure

itami *n.* pain

itamu *v.i. I.* to ache

itashi-masu to do (respectful form of suru)

ito *n.* thread

itsu *adv.* when? (19)

itsuka five days, fifth day (36)

itsuka some time, some other time

itsu-kumi five sets (32)

itsumo *adv.* always (15)

itsutsu *numeral* five (29)

itsuwari *n.* deception

itsuwaru *v.t. I.* to deceive

itta went (past form of iku)(40)

itte-kuru to take a round trip, to have been to (24)

iu *v.i. v.t. I.* to say, to call (38)

iya-na *n-adj.* disagreeable

iyashii *adj.* vulgar

J

jama *n.* obstruction, interruption

jari *n.* gravel

ji *n.* letter, character, ideograph

ji *n.* time, hour, o'clock (35)

jibiki *n.* dictionary

jibun *n.* self

jidoo (*adj.*) automatic

jidoosha *n.* automobile (52)

jikan *n.* time, hour (35)

jiki-ni *adv.* soon

jiman *n.* pride

jimen *n.* ground

jimusho *n.* office (52)

jippai ten (cup)-fuls (32)

jippiki ten " heads " (32)

jippon ten " sticks " (32)

jippun ten minutes (35)

jishin *n.* earthquake

jishin *pron.* self

jisho *n.* dictionary

jissai *n. n-adj.* fact, real (jissai-no)

jissatsu ten volumes (32)

jissen ten sen (35)

jitensha *n.* bicycle (52)

jiyuu *n.* liberty

jiyuu-na *n-adj.* free

jochuu *n.* maid servant

joodan *n.* joke

joohin-na *n-adj.* genteel

jooki *n.* steam

joomae *n.* lock

jo-oo *n.* queen

jootai *n.* condition, circumstance

joozu-na *n-adj.* skilful

junban *n.* turn, sequence

junjo *n.* order, sequence

junsa *n.* police man

juu *numeral* ten (30)

juubun-na *n-adj.* enough

Juu-gatsu October (36)

Juu-ichi-gatsu November (36)

juu-ippon eleven " sticks " (32

juu-ippun eleven minutes (35)

juu-issatsu eleven volumes (33)

Juu-ni-gatsu December (36)

K

ka *n.* mosquito

ka *adv.* ? (2)

kaban *n.* bag, suitcase

kabe *n.* wall (16, 54)

kachi *n.* victory

kado *n.* corner

kaeri *n.* return, way back

kaeru *v.i. I.* to return

kaeru *v.t. II.* to change, to substitute

kaetta returned (past form of kaeru) (40)

kagaku *n.* science

kagaku *n.* chemistry

kagami *n.* mirror

kagayaku *v.i. I.* to shine

kage *n.* shadow, shade

kagi *n.* key

kagiri *n.* limit

kagiru *v.t. I.* to limit

kago *n.* basket

kagu *v.t. I.* to smell

kai *suf.* floor, storey (52)

kai *n.* shell-fish

kaigan *n.* seashore

kaigun *n.* navy

kaikei *n.* accounts, accountant

kaiko *n.* silkworm

kaisha *n.* company, corporation

kaita wrote (past form of kaku (40)

kaji *n.* fire (house on fire)

kakaru *v.i. I.* to hang, to cost

kakemono *n.* hanging scroll

kakeru *v.i. v.t. II.* to run (42)

kakeru *v.t. II.* to hang, to spend

kakeru *v.i. II.* to sit on

kako *n.* past

kakoi *n.* enclosure, fence

kakomu *v.t. I.* to surround

kaku *n.* angle

kaku *v.t. I.* to write, to scratch (23)

kakureru *v.i. II.* to hide

kakusu *v.t. I.* to hide

kama *n.* kettle, boiler

kami *n.* paper (31)

kaminari *n.* thunder

kami-sama *n.* god

kamoku *n.* subject, branch of study

kamu *v.t. I.* to bite, to chew

kana *n.* syllabary, Japanese syllabic letters

kanarazu *adv.* surely, without fail

kanashii *adj.* sad

kanashimi *n.* sorrow

kanashimu *v.t. I.* to grieve

kane *n.* metal, money

kangae *n.* thought, idea

kangaeru *v.t. II.* to think

kangei *n.* welcome

kanji *n.* feeling, sense

kanjiru *v.t. II.* to feel

kanjoo *n.* counting, accounts

kanjoo-suru *v.t. irr.* to count

kankei *n.* relation

kantan-na *n-adj.* simple

kanzen *n.* perfection

kanzen-na *n-adj.* perfect

kao *n.* face, countenance

kara *postp.* from, since (19)

kara *con.* therefore, because (47)

kara *n., n-adj.* empty (kara-na)

karada *n.* body

karai *adj.* salty, hot (peppery)

kare *pron.* he

kari-no *n-adj.* temporary, substitute

kariru *v.t. II.* to borrow

karui *adj.* light in weight

kasa *n.* umbrella

kasanaru *v.i. I.* to be piled up, to be repeated

kasaneru *v.t. II.* to pile up, to repeat

kashi *n.* cake, confectionery

kashi *n.* loan, lending

kashira *n.* head, headman

kasu *v.t. I.* to lend

kasuka-na *n-adj.* faint, dim

kata *n.* shoulder

kata *n.* type, style, mould

katachi *n.* shape

katai *adj.* hard, firm

katana *n.* sword

kata-sa *n.* degree of hardness

katazukeru *v.t. II.* to put in order

katei *n.* home, family

katsu *v.i. I.* to win

katta won (past form of **katsu**)

katta bought (past form of **kau**)

katte *n. & n-adj.* one's own way, wilful

kau *v.t. I.* to buy (21)

kawa *n.* skin

kawa *n.* river

kawaita *(adj.)* dry

kawakasu *v.t. I.* to dry

kawaku *v.i. I.* to dry

kawari *n. & n-adj.* substitute

kawaru *v.i. I.* to change, to take the place of

Kayoobi *n.* Tuesday (36)

kayui *adj.* itchy

kazari *n.* decoration

kazaru *v.t. I.* to decorate

kaze *n.* wind

kazoeru *v.t. II.* to count (52)

kazu *n.* number

ke *n.* hair

kechi-na *n-adj.* stingy

kega *n.* injury, wound

keikaku *n.* plan

keikaku-suru *v.t. irr.* to plan

keiken *n.* experience

keiken-suru *v.t. irr.* to experience

keisatsu *n.* police

keizai *n.* economy, economics

kekka *n.* result

kekkon *n.* marriage

kekkon-suru *v.i. irr.* to marry

kemu, kemuri *n.* smoke

ken *n.* prefecture

ken-i *n.* authority

kenkoo *n.* health

kenri *n.* right, claim

keredomo *con.* but (14)

keru *v.t. I.* to kick

ki *n.* tree, wood (10, 39,)

kibishii *adj.* severe, strict

kichigai *n.* insane person

kiiro *n.* yellow

kiiroi *adj.* yellow

kikai *n.* chance

kikai *n.* machine

kiken *n.* danger. **kiken-na** *n-adj.* dangerous

kikoeru *v.i. II.* to be audible, to sound

kiku *v.t. I.* to hear, to listen to

kimari *n.* regulation

kimaru *v.i. I.* to be decided

ki-masu come (19)

kimeru *v.t. II.* to decide

kimono *n.* clothing (4)

kin *n.* gold

kinen *n.* memorial (54)

kinoo *n.* yesterday (19, 36)

kinu *n.* silk

Kin-yoobi *n.* Friday (36)

kinzoku *n. & n-adj.* metal

kioku *n.* memory

kioku-suru *v.t. irr.* to remember

kippu *n.* ticket (27)

kirai-na *n-adj.* distasteful

kirau *v.t. I.* to dislike

kire *n.* cloth

kirei-na *n-adj.* pretty, clean (6)

kireru *(adj.)* sharp

kireru *v.i. II.* to be cut, to be severed

kiri *n.* fog, mist

kiroku *n.* record, document

kiroku-suru *v.t. irr.* to record

kiru *v.t. I.* to cut

kiru *v.t. II.* to wear, to put on

kisen *n.* steamer

kisha *n.* railway train (50)

kisoku *n.* rule, regulation

kita *n.* north

ki-ta came (past form of **kuru**) (41)

kitanai *adj.* ugly, dirty (6)

kitte *n.* postage stamp

ko *n.* child (42, 51)

ko *suf.* piece

kochira *pron.* here

kodomo *n.* child (33)

koe *n.* voice

koeru *v.t. II.* to go over, to surmount

koi come (imperative form of **kuru**)

koi *n.* carp fish (46)

koi-nobori *n.* carp streamer (46)

kojiki *n.* beggar

koke *n.* moss

koko *pron.* here (9)

kokonoka nine days, ninth day of the month (36)

kokonotsu *numeral* nine (29)

kokoro *n.* mind, heart

kokoromiru *v.t. II.* to try

kokorozashi *n.* intention

kokorozasu *v.t. I.* to intend

kokusai *n-adj.* international

komaru *v.i. I.* to be troubled

kome *n.* rice, rice grain

kona *n.* powder, flour

ko-nai do not come (43)

kon-getsu this month (36)

kon-nen this year (36)

kon-nichi today (36)

kono *(adj.)* this (8)

konomi *n.* liking, taste

konomu *v.t. I.* to like, to have a taste for

kon-shuu this week (36)

kooen *n.* park

koogeki *n.* attack

koogeki-suru *v.t. irr.* to attack

Koogoo *n.* Empress

koogyoo *n.* industry

koohii *n.* coffee

koojoo *n.* factory

kookoku *n.* advertisement

kookoku-suru *v.t. irr.* to advertise

koori *n.* ice

ko-rareru can come

kore *pron.* this (1)

koro *n. & suf.* time, about the time

ko-saseru let someone come (50)

koshi *n.* hip, waist

kosuru *v.t. I.* to rub

kotae *n.* answer

kotaeru *v.i. II.* to answer

koto *n.* matter, thing, fact (37, 48)

kotoba *n.* word, speech, language

kotoshi this year (36)

kowai *adj.* fearful

kowasu *v.t. I.* to break up (25, 49)

koyomi *n.* calendar

koyoo will come (future form of kuru) (41)

ku *numeral* nine (30)

kubi *n.* neck, head

kuchi *n.* mouth, entrance

kuchibiru *n.* lip

kuchi-e *n.* frontispiece (42)

kudakeru *v.i. II.* to shatter into pieces   ⌊pieces

kudaku *v.t. I.* to shatter into

kudamono *n.* fruit

kudasai (imperative) please give the favour of (27)

kudasaru *v.t. I.* to give, (to send down)

kudasatta gave (past form of kudasaru) (40)

Ku-gatsu September (36)

kugi *n.* nail, spike

kuki *n.* stalk, stem

kumi *n.* class, group

kumi *suf.* set, pair (32)

kumo *n.* cloud

kumo *n.* spider

kun *suf.* Mr.

kuni *n.* country, nation

kurabu *n.* club, association

kurai *adj.* dark

kuro *n.* black.   kuroi *adj.* black

kuru *v.i. irr.* come (19, 41)

kuruma *n.* car

kuruma *n.* wheel

kurushimi *n.* suffering, hard- ship   ⌈fe:

kurushimu *v.i. & v.t. I.* to suf·

kurushii *adj.* painful, hard

kusa *n.* grass

kusari *n.* chain

kusaru *v.i. I.* to rot

kushi *n.* comb

kusuri *n.* medicine, chemical

kutsu *n.* shoes, boots (39)

kuuki *n.* air

kuwa *n.* hoe

kuyamu *v.t. I.* to regret

kyaku guest (o-kyaku) (16)

kyoku *n.* office, bureau

kyo-nen last year (36)

kyoo *n.* today (36)

kyooiku *n.* education

kyooiku-suru *v.t. irr.* to educate

kyoomi *n.* interest, liking

kyuu *n.* grade, class

kyuu *numeral* nine

M

machi *n.* town, street (52)

mada *adv.* yet, not yet (42)

made *postp.* till, as far as (20, 35)

mado *n.* window (15)

mae *n.* front, before, ago (12, 35)

magaru *v.i. I.* to bend, to turn

magatta (*adj.*) crooked

mageru *v.t. II.* to bend

mai *suf.* sheet of (31)

mai *pref.* every, each

majime-na *n-adj.* serious, earnest

makoto *n.* sincerity. makoto-no *n-adj.* sincere

maku *v.t. I.* to roll, to wind

mama *postp.* as, same

mame *n.* beans, peas

mamoru *v.t. I.* to defend, to keep

man *numeral* ten thousand (30)

manzoku *n.* satisfaction. manzoku-na *n-adj.* satisfactory

manzoku-suru *v.i. irr.* to be satisfied

maru *n.* circle

marui *adj.* round

masatsu *n.* friction

-masen do not (negative form of masu) (3)

-masen-deshita did not (past negative form of masu) (19)

-masen-deshoo will not, shall not (future negative form of masu) (22)

-mashita suffix for past tense (past form of masu) (19)

-mashoo will, shall, let us (future form of masu) (21, 22)

-masu *auxil. v.* " do " (3, 17)

mata *adv.* again, also

matsu *n.* pine tree (46)

matsu *v.t. I.* to wait

matsuri *n.* festival

mattaku *adv.* quite, entirely

mawari *n.* circumference, neighbourhood

mazaru *v.i. I.* to become mixed

mazeru *v.t. II.* to mix

me *n.* eye

me *n.* sprout, bud

medetai *adj.* happy, worthy of congratulation

megane *n.* spectacles

meetoru *n.* meter

meetoru metre (unit of length)

mesu *n. & n-adj.* female

mi *n.* fruit, nut

michi *n.* road, way, method

michiru *v.i. II.* to become full

midori *n.* green (midori-no)

mieru *v.i. II.* to be visible

migaku *v.t. I.* to polish

migaita *(adj.)* polished

migi *n. & n-adj.* right (12)

mijikai *adj.* short

miki *n.* tree-trunk

mikka three days, third day of the month (36)

mikumi three sets (32)

mimi *n.* ear

minami *n.* south

minato *n.* harbour, port

minikui *adj.* ugly

miru *v.t. II.* to see (18)

misoka last day of the month (36)

mitasu *v.t. I.* to fill

mi-te-miru look and see, examine (24)

mittsu *numeral* three (28)

mizu *n.* water (21)

mo *postp.* also

mochi-masu have, hold (18)

mokuteki *n.* object, purpose

Mokuyoobi *n.* Thursday (36)

mon *n.* gate

mono *n.* thing (13)

mono *n.* person

moo *adv.* already, more (43)

moo hitotsu one more, another (49)

morau *v.t. I.* to receive, to be given

moshi —naraba if

moshimo —kereba if (53)

moshimo —naraba if

moshi-moshi hello (a call)

moto *n.* basis, origin, root

motsu *v.t. I.* to hold, to have (18)

motte *adv.* with, by

motte-iku take, take away (24)

motte-kuru bring (24)

motto *adv.* more (34)

muchi *n.* whip

mugi *n.* wheat

muika six days, sixth day of the month (36)

muku *v.t. I.* to peel, to skin

mukui *n.* reward

mu-kumi six sets (32)

mune *n.* chest, breast, mind

mura *n.* village

murasaki *n.* purple (murasaki-no)

mure *n.* crowd, flock

muri-na *n-adj.* unreasonable

musha-ningyoo *n.* warrior dolls (46)

mushi *n.* insect, worm

musubi *n.* tie, knot, end

musubu *v.t. I.* to tie, to conclude

muttsu *numeral* six (29)

muzukashii *adj.* difficult

muzukashi-sa *n.* difficulty (the degree of)

myoo-nen next year (36)

myoo-nichi *n.* tomorrow (36)

N

-na " of " (ending for noun-adjective) (6)

na *n.* name (54)

nabe *n.* pan, pot

nado *suf.* and the like, etc.

nagai *adj.* long (54)

nagame *n.* view, scenery

nagameru *v.t. II.* to view, to look at

nagara *suf., adv.* while, as though

nagare *n.* stream

nagareru *v.i. II.* to flow

naga-sa *n.* length

nagasu *v.t. I.* to let flow, to shed

nagusami *n.* recreation

nagusameru *v.t. II.* to console

nai *v.i. irr.* is not, are not, am not (negative form of aru) (45)

nai *adj., auxil. v.* not, un-, in-, (13)

naka *n.* inside, between, middle (11, 42)

nakaroo will not be, shall not be (future negative of **aru**) (45)

nakatta was not, were not (past negative of **aru**) (45)

naka-yoshi *n.* good friends, chums (42)

-nakereba naranai must (53)

naku *v.i. I.* to cry, to weep

namae *n.* name (54)

nameraka-na *n-adj.* smooth

nami *n.* wave

nan *adj., pron.* what? (2)

nanatsu *numeral* seven (29)

nan-bai how many (cup)-fuls? (32) ⌈(32)

nan-biki how many "heads"?

nan-bon how many "sticks"? (32)

nan-gatsu what month? (36)

nani *pron.* what? (2)

nani-mo (not) anything (27)

nani-yoobi what day of the week?

nan-ji what time? (35)

nan-ka-getsu how many months? (36)

nan-nichi what day? how many days? (36)

nan-shuukan how many weeks?

nanuka seven days, seventh day of the month (36)

nao *adv.* more, also ⌈recover

naoru *v.i. I.* to be corrected, to

naosu *v.t. I.* to correct, to cure

nara-nai will not do (must)

nareru *v.i. II.* to become accustomed, to grow skilful

nareru *v.i. II.* to become tame

nareta (*adj.*) accustomed, familiar

nareta (*adj.*) tame ⌈(46, 54)

naru *v.i. I.* to become, to grow

natsu *n.* summer

ne *n.* root

negai *n.* wish, request

negau *v.t. I.* to wish, to request

negi *n.* onion

neji *n.* screw, bolt, nut

nejireru *v.i. II.* to become twisted

nejireta (*adj.*) twisted

nejiru *v.t. I.* to twist

neko *n.* cat

nemuru *v.i. I.* to sleep

nen *n., suf.* year

neru *v.i. II.* to lie down, to sleep

netsu *n.* heat, fever

nezumi *n.* rat, mouse

ni *numeral* two (30)

-ni *postp.* to, in, on, at (9, 27)

nibui *adj.* dull, slow

nichi *n. suf.* day (36)

Nichiyoobi *n.* Sunday (36)

nigai *adj.* bitter

Ni-gatsu February (32)

nigiru *v.t. I.* to grip, to hold

nigori *n.* muddiness, turbidity

nigoru *v.i. I.* to become muddy

nigosu *v.t. I.* to make muddy

nigotta (*adj.*) muddy, impure

ni-jissatsu twenty volumes (32)

niku *n.* meat, flesh (23)

nikui *adj.* detestable

nikumu *v.t. I.* to hate

nikurashii *adj.* detestable

nin *suf.* man, number of men (32)

ningyoo *n.* doll

nioi *n.* smell

niou *v.i. I.* to smell

Nippon *n.* Japan (15)

niru *v.i. II.* to resemble

niru *v.t. II.* to boil

nise-no *n-adj.* counterfeit

nishi *n.* west

niwa *n.* yard, garden (10)

niwatori *n.* chicken

-no *postp.* of (4)

nobasu *v.t. I.* to stretch, to let grow

nobiru *v.i. II.* to grow, to stretch

nochi *n., n-adj.* later, future

nodo *n.* throat

nohara *n.* field

-no mae-ni in front of (12)

nomi *n.* flea

nomu *v.t. I.* to drink

-no naka-de in, among (34)

-no naka-ni in, inside (11)

noo *n.* brain

noogyoo *n.* agriculture

nori *n.* paste

noru *v.i. I.* to ride (21)

-no shita-ni under (11)

notta rode (past form of noru)

-no ue-ni on, upon (11)

-no ushiro-ni behind (12)

nozomi *n.* hope

nozomu *v.t. I.* to hope

-nu *auxil. v.* not

nuno *n.* cloth

nusumu *v.t. I.* to steal

O

o *n.* tail

o- *honorific pref.* honorable

oba *n.* aunt

obi *n.* belt, sash

oboe *n.* memory

oboeru *v.t. II.* to remember, to memorize (40)

o-cha *n.* tea (16)

odori *n.* dance

odoroku *v.i. I.* to be surprised

odoru *v.t. I.* to dance

o-hashi *n.* chop-sticks

o-hitsu *n.* rice tub (26)

oite *postp.* at, in, on

oji *n.* uncle

o-kashi *n.* cake, sweets (44)

oki-mono *n.* ornament to be set on tokonoma and shelves (16)

okiru *v.i. II.* to get up

okosu *v.t. I.* to raise up, to arouse

oku *v.t. I.* to place, to leave (46)

oku *n.* inner part, back room

oku *numeral* hundred million (30)

okuru *v.t. I.* to send

oku-san, oku-sama *n.* wife, mistress of a house (39)

o-kyaku *n.* guest (16, 39)
o-matsuri *n.* festival (46)
omoi *n-adj.* heavy
omo-sa *n.* weight
omoshiroi *adj.* interesting (51)
omote *n.* *n-adj.* front, front face, out of doors
omou *v.t. I.* to think (42)
onaji *n-adj.* same
ongaku *n.* music
onna, onna-no hito *n.* woman (42)
onna-no ko *n.* girl (42)
oo, oo-sama *n.* king
ooi *adj.* many, much
ookii *adj.* big (5)
ookiku naru to grow
ooki-sa *n.* size
ooyake-no *n-adj.* public
oreru *v.i. II.* to become bent, folded, or broken
ori-mono *n.* cloth, woven thing
oru *v.t. I.* to bend, to fold, to break
oru *v.t. I.* to weave
oru *v.i. I.* to be
oshie *n.* teaching, precept (38)
oshieru *v.t. II.* to teach (38)
osoi *adj.* slow, late
osore *n.* fear
osoreru *v.t. II.* to fear
osu *v.t. I.* to push
osu *n.,* *n-adj.* male
oto *n.* sound, noise
otoko, otoko-no hito *n.* man (1)
otoko-no ko *n.* boy (42)

otooto *n.* younger brother
otoru *v.i. I.* to be inferior
o-wan *n.* wooden bowl (26)
owari *n.* end
owaru *v.i.,* *v.t. I.* to end, to finish
oyogu *v.t. I.* to swim

P

pan *n.* bread
peiji *n.,* *suf.* page
penki *n.* paint
pokketto *n.* pocket
ponpu *n.* pump

R

-ra *suf.* used after nouns and pronouns to indicate plurality
rai-getsu next month (36)
rai-nen next year (36)
rai-shuu next week (36)
rajio *n.* radio
raku *n.* ease, comfort
raku-suru *v.i. irr.* to take it easy, to be comfortable
-rareru *auxil. v.* to be able, & passive voice (47, 49)
rashii *postp.,* *adj.* apparently, as if
rei *n.* zero (30)
rei *n.* example
rei *n.* salutation, thanks
reigi *n.* etiquette
rei-suru *v.i. irr.* to bow, to greet
rekishi *n.* history
renga *n.* brick
renmei *n.* league

renraku *n*. communication, connection

renraku-suru *v.i. irr*. to make contact

retsu *n*. rank, column

rieki *n*. profit

rikoo-na *n-adj*. intelligent, wise (13)

riku *n*. land

rikugun *n*. army

ringo *n*. apple

rippa-na *n-adj*. fine, magnificent (7)

rittoru litre (unit of measure)

riyuu *n*. reason, ground

roku *numeral* six (30)

Roku-gatsu June (36)

ron *n*. argument

roppai six (cup) fuls (32)

roppiki six " heads " (32)

roppon six " sticks " (32)

roppun six minutes (35)

rui *n*. kind, sort

ryoori *n*. cooking

ryoori-suru *v.t. irr*. to cook

ryuukoo *n*. fashion, fad

ryuukoo-suru *v.i. irr*. to be in fashion

S

sabi *n*. rust, corrosion

sabiru *v.i. II*. to rust, to corrode

sadamaru *v.i. I*. to be fixed, to become settled

sadame *n*. regulation, rule

sadameru *v.t. II*. to fix, to settle

sae *postp*. even, only

-sai *suf*. year old as ni-sai＝two years old (36)

saiban *n*. trial, judgment

saiban-suru *v.t. irr*. to pass judgment

saiwai *n*. happiness. saiwai-na *n-adj*. happy, lucky

saka *n*. hill, slope

sakai *n*. border, boundary

sakana *n*. fish (46)

sakasama *n., n-adj*. upside down, inverted

sake *n*. wine, liquor

sakeru *v.t. II*. to avoid

sakeru *v.i. II*. to tear

saku *v.t. I*. to tear

sakujitsu *n*. yesterday (36)

saku-nen last year (36)

sakura *n*. cherry blossom, tree

sama *suf*. Mr., Mrs., Miss

samatage *n*. obstruction

samatageru *v.t. II*. to obstruct

samui *adj*. cold

samu-sa *n*. degree of coldness

san *numeral* three

san *suf*. Mr., Mrs., Miss (3)

san *n*. acid

san-bai three (cup) fuls (32)

san-biki three " heads " (32)

san-bon three " sticks " (32)

San-gatsu March (36)

san-pun three minutes (35)

sansei *n*. approval

sansei-suru *v.t. v.i. irr*. to approve

sara *n.* tray, dish (26)

saseru *v.t. II.* to let someone do (50)

-saseru *auxil. v.* to let, to make (causative) (50)

sasou *v.t. I.* to invite, to entice

satoo *n.* sugar

satsu *n.* paper-money, bank-note

-satsu *suf.* for counting books, volume (31)

sawagu *v.t. I.* to be excited, to make noise

sayonara goodbye (39)

seifu *n.* government.

seikaku *n.* character, nature

seikatsu *n.* life, living

seikatsu-suru *v.i. irr.* to live, to make living

seikoo *n.* success

seikoo-suru *v.i. irr.* to succeed

seimitsu *n. n-adj.* precision, precise (seimitsu-na)

seiri *n.* arrangement, order

seiri-suru *v.t. irr.* to arrange, to put in order

seishin *n.* spirit

seishitsu *n.* character, nature

seiyoo *n. n-adj.* Europe, European

seiyoo-jin *n.* European

sekai *n.* world

seki *n.* seat

seki *n.* cough

sekinin *n.* responsibility

seki-suru *v.i. irr.* to cough

sekitan *n.* coal

sekiyu *n.* kerosene, petroleum

semai *adj.* narrow, small in area (7)

semento *n.* cement

sen *n.* line

sen unit of money, 100 sen make one yen (35)

sen *numeral* thousand (30)

sen-getsu last month (36)

senkyo *n.* election

sensei *n.* teacher (49)

sensoo *n.* war

sen-shuu last week (36)

sentaku *n.* wash, laundry

sentaku-suru *v.t. irr.* to launder, to wash

se-rareru can do (47)

setomono *n.* chinaware

setsumei *n.* explanation

setsumei-suru *v.t. irr.* to explain

shabon *n.* soap

shakai *n.* society

shakai-gaku *n.* sociology

shakai-teki *(adj.)* social

shashin *n.* photograph (46)

shatsu *n.* under-shirt (6)

shi *n.* city

shi *numeral* four (30)

shichi *numeral* seven (36)

Shichi-gatsu July (36)

shidoo *n.* leading, direction

shidoo-sha *n.* leader

shidoo-suru *v.t. irr.* to lead, to direct

Shi-gatsu April (36)

shigeki *n.* stimulus, excitement

shigeki-suru *v.t. irr.* to excite, to stimulate

shigoto *n.* work

shigoto-suru *v.i. irr.* to work

shihai *n.* management

shihai-nin *n.* manager

shihai-suru *v.t. irr.* to manage

shikake *n.* device, mechanism

shikakeru *v.t. II.* to make a device

shikaru *v.t. I.* to scold, to reprimand

shikashi *con.*but

shi-masu do (17, 40)

shimatta finished, put away (past form of shimau) (40)

shimau *v.t. I.* to finish, to put away

shimeru *v.t. II.* to close (17)

shimeru *v.t. I.* to become moist

shimetta (*adj.*) wet, damp

shina *n.* thing, article

shi-nai do not do (43)

shinbun *n.* newspaper (17)

shinchuu *n.* brass

shinjiru *v.t. II.* to believe

shinkei *n.* nerve, nervous system

shinpai *n.* anxiety

shinpai-suru *v.t. irr.* to worry

shinsetsu *n.* kindness. shinsetsu-na *n-adj.* kind (13)

shinu *v.i. I.* die (54)

shinzoo *n.* heart

shio *n.* salt

shippai *n.* failure

shippai-suru *v.i. irr.* to fail

shi-rareru be known, become known

shi-rareru can do, be done (47, 49)

shirase *n.* report

shiraseru *v.t. II.* to report, to notify

shireru *v.i. II.* to become known

shiro *n.* white. sihroi *adj.* white

shiru *n.* juice, soup

shiru *v.t. I.* to know

shirushi *n.* mark, sign

shita *n.* tongue

shita *n.* lower part, under side

shi-ta did (past form of suru)

shitagaeru *v.t. II.* to subjugate, to be attended by

shitagau *v.i. I.* to obey

shitashii *adj.* intimate

shi-te-miru do and see, try (24)

shitsu *n.* room

shitsu *n.* nature, quality

shitsukkoi *adj.* obstinate

shiyoo will do (future form of suru) (41)

shizen *n.* nature. shizen-no *n-adj.* natural

shizuka-na *n-adj.* quiet

shizuke-sa *n.* quietness, stillness

shokubutsu *n.* plant, plant life

shokumin *n.* colonization

shokumin-suru *v.i. irr.* to colonize

shoo *n.* chapter

shoo will be, shall be (contraction of ari-mashoo) (22)

shooji *n.* paper door with single layer of light paper (15)

shookai *n.* introduction

shookai-suru *v.t. irr.* to introduce

shooko *n.* proof, evidence

shookoo *n.* military officer

shoosetsu *n.* novel

shujin *n.* master, mistress, host

shujutsu *n.* operation (medical)

shuu, shuukan *n.* week (36)

shuukan *n.* custom

shuukyoo *n.* religion

soba *n.* side (12)

sode *n.* sleeve

soeru *v.t. II.* to add, to attach

soko *pron.* there (9)

sonkei *n.* respect

sonkei-suru *v.t. irr.* to respect

sono *(adj.)* that (8)

soo *adv.* so (3)

soodan *n.* consultation

soozoo *n.* imagination

sora *n.* sky

sore *pron.* that (1)

sosen *n.* ancestor

soshiki *n.* system

soshite *con.* and (14)

soto *n.* outside, out doors

su is, are, am (contraction of ari-masu) (1)

suberu *v.t. I.* to slip, to slide

subete *n., n-adj.* all

sugi *suf.* past

sugiru *v.t. II.* to pass

sugu *adv.* at once (47)

sugureru *v.i. II.* to excel

sugureta *(adj.)* excellent

suidoo *n.* water-works

suidoo-sen *n.* hydrant, watertap

Suiyoobi *n.* Wednesday (36)

suji *n.* line, sinew

suki *n-adj.* fond of, like (52)

sukoshi *n-adj.* a little, some (44)

sukoshi-mo not any (44)

sumai *n.* dwelling

sumau *v.i. I.* to dwell

sumi *n.* charcoal

sumi *n.* Indian ink

sumoo *n.* wrestling

sumoo-wo toru to wrestle

sumu *v.i. I.* to live, to dwell (54)

sumu *v.i. I.* to finish

suna *n.* sand

sunda lived, resided (past form of sumu) (54)

sunda finished (past form of sumu)

suru *v.t. irr.* to do (17, 41)

surudoi *adj.* sharp

surudo-sa *n.* sharpness

susumeru *v.t. II.* to advance, to recommend, to encourage

suteru *v.t. II.* to throw away

suu *n.* number

suu *v.t. I.* to suck

suwaru *v.i. I.* to sit, to sit on the floor (18)

suwatta sat (past form of suwa-ru) (18)

suzushii *adj.* cool

suzushi-sa *n.* coolness

T

^ta *n.* paddy field

-ta verb ending for past tense (40)

ta *n.* other, others

taba *n.* bunch

tabako *n.* tobacco (16)

tabako-bon *n.* tobacco tray (16)

taberu *v.t. II.* to eat

tabi *n.* travel

tachi *n.* nature, quality

tachi-masu stand (tatsu) (18)

tada *adv.* only

tada-no *n-adj.* common, free of charge

tadashii *adj.* right, honest

tagai-no, o-tagai-no *n-adj.* mutual

tai *adj.* desirous of (52)

taido *n.* attitude

taihen *adv.* very, unusually (14)

taira-na *n-adj.* flat, smooth (6)

taisetsu-na *n-adj.* important, precious (6)

takai *adj.* high, tall, expensive (13, 34)

taka-sa *n.* heigh

take *n.* bamboo

taku *n.* house, home

takusan-no *n-adj.* many, much (29)

takuwae *n.* savings, store

takuwaeru *v.t. II.* to save, to store

tama *n.* ball, precious stone

tamago *n.* egg

tame *n.* benefit, sake. tame-ni *adv.* for the sake of, in order that (54)

tana *n.* shelf (9)

tane *n.* seed

tani *n.* valley

tan-i *n.* unit

tanjun-na *n-adj.* simple

tanomi *n.* request

tanomu *v.t. I.* to request

tanoshii *adj.* pleasant

tanoshimi *n.* pleasure, recreation

tanoshimu *v.t. I.* to enjoy

tansu *n.* chest of drawers

taoreru *v.i. II.* to topple over

taosu *v.t. I.* to overthrow

tarai *n.* basin, tub

tarasu *v.t. I.* to let drip, to spill

tareru *v.i. II.* to drip

tariru *v.i. II.* to be enough

tashika-na *n-adj.* certain, sure

tasuke *n.* help

tasukeru *v.t. II.* to help

tatakai *n.* battle, war

tatakau *v.i. I.* to fight

tatami *n.* reed mat, matted floor (15)

tate-no *n-adj.* length-wise, vertical

tateru *v.t. II.* to set up

tatsu *v.i. I.* to stand (18)

tatta stood (past form of tatsu)

te *n.* hand

-te *postp.* and

tegami *n.* letter (23, 38)

Teikoku *n., n-adj.* Empire, Imperial (54)

Teikoku Daigaku Imperial University (54)

teishaba *n.* railway station

teki *n.* enemy

-teki *suf.* -ic, -ous (added to a noun to form adjective)

tekitoo-na *n-adj.* appropriate

ten *n.* point, mark

tenjoo *n.* ceiling (16)

tenki *n.* weather

Tennoo *n.* Japanese Emperor

teppoo *n.* gun

tetsu *n.* iron

-tewa nara-nai must not (53)

to *n.* door (28)

to *postp.* and (4)

to *con.* " that " (38)

tobu *v.i. v.t. I.* to fly

todana *n.* closet, cupboard (11)

todokeru *v.t. II.* to report, to deliver

todoku *v.i. I.* to reach

toi *n.* question

tojiru *v.t. II.* to close

tojiru *v.t. II.* to bind (as a book)

tokei *n.* clock, watch

tokeru *v.i. II.* to melt, to loosen, to become untied

toki *n.* time (39)

toko *n.* bed

tokonoma *n.* alcove (16)

tokoro *n.* place (39)

toku *n.* virtue

toku *n.* profit

toku *v.t. I.* to melt, to solve, to untie

tokubetsu-no *n-adj.* special

to-kumi ten sets, ten pairs (32)

tomaru *v.i. I.* to stop

tomeru *v.t. II.* to stop

tomo-dachi *n.* friend

tomu *v.i. I.* to be rich

tonari-no *n-adj.* neighbouring (46)

tonda *(adj.)* rich

too *n.* tower

too *numeral* ten (29)

tooi *adj.* far (51)

tooka ten days, tenth day (36)

toori *n.* street

tooru *v.t. I.* to pass, to go along

too-sa *n.* distance

toosu *v.t. I.* to let pass, to push through

tori *n.* bird, chicken

toru *v.t. I.* to take, to take off, to catch (23, 39)

toshi *n.* year, age (36)

toshokan *n.* library

totsuzen *n., n-adj.* sudden

totta took, took off, (past form of **toru**) (39)

tou *v.t. I.* to inquire

tsubomi *n.* bud, budding flower

tsubu *n.* grain, particle

tsuchi *n.* soil, earth

tsue *n.* cane, stick

tsugi *n.* next. tsugi-no *n-adj.* next

tsugoo *n.* convenience, circumstance

tsugoo-suru *v.t. irr.* to arrange, to accommodate

tsuitachi first day of the month (36)

tsuitate *n.* standing screen (39)

tsuite *con.* of, concerning

tsukaeru *v.i. II.* to serve, to wait upon

tsukaeru *v.i. II.* to be obstructed, to be clogged

tsukai *n.* messenger

tsukare *n.* fatigue

tsukareru *v.i. II.* to be tired

tsukareta *(adj.)* tired

tsukatta used, employed (past form of tsukau) (40)

tsukau *v.t. I.* to use, to employ (37)

tsukeru *v.t. II.* to attach

tsuki *n.* moon, month (36)

tsuku *v.i. I.* to stick

tsuku *v.i. I.* to arrive

tsuku *v.t. I.* to push, to stab

tsukue *n.* desk, table (15)

tsukuru *v.t. I.* to make, to create (25, 49)

tsuma *n.* wife

tsume *n.* finger nail, claw

tsumi *n.* sin, crime

tsunagu *v.t. I.* to connect, to tie

tsuno *n.* horn

tsutome *n.* work

tsutomeru *v.i. v.t. II.* to serve as, to work at

tsutsumi *n.* bundle, wrapping

tsutsumu *v.t. I.* to wrap

tsuushin *n.* correspondence, report

tsuushin-suru *v.t. irr.* to report, to correspond

tsuyoi *adj.* strong (46)

tsuyo-sa *n.* strength

tsuyu *n.* dew, juice

U

uchi *n.* inside

uchi *n.* house (14)

ue *n.* top, topside (11)

ukeru *v.t. II.* to receive

uma *n.* horse

umareru *v.i. II.* to be born

umaru *v.i. I.* to become buried

umeru *v.t. II.* to bury

umi *n.* sea

undoo *n.* exercise, motion

undoo-suru *v.i. irr.* to exercise, to move

ura *n.* back side, reverse side

uru *v.t. I.* to sell

ushi *n.* cow, ox

ushiro *n.* back, backside (12)

uso *n.* lie

usui *adj.* thin in thickness, light in colour

uta *n.* song, poem

utagai *n.* doubt, suspicion
utagau *v.t. I.* to doubt
utau *v.t. I.* to sing
utsu *v.t. I.* to strike, to shoot
utsukushii *adj.* beautiful
utsukushi-sa *n.* beauty
uzumaru *v.i. I.* to become buried
uzumeru *v.t. II.* to bury

W

wa *n.* circle, ring
wa ending for subject (1)
wakai *adj.* young
wakareru *v.i. II.* to part
wakaru *v.i. I.* to understand, to be understandable
wakasu *v.t. I.* to boil
wakeru *v.t. II.* to divide
waku *v.i. I.* to boil
waku *n.* frame
warau *v.t. I.* to laugh, to smile
wariai *n.* percentage, rate, ratio
waru *v.t. I.* to break, to crack
warui *adj.* bad (5)
wasureru *v.t. II.* to forget (25)
wata *n.* cotton
watakushi *pron.* I (1)
wazuka-no *n-adj.* few, little
-wo ending for object (17, 27)

Y

ya *n.* arrow
ya *postp.* and, also
yadoya *n.* inn, hotel
yaku *v.t. I.* to burn

yaku *n.* office, post
ya-kumi eight sets, eight pairs (32)
yakusho *n.* public office
yama *n.* mountain
yameru *v.t. II.* to stop, to give up
yane *n.* roof
yasai *n.* vegetables
yaseru *v.i. II.* to grow thin
yaseta (*adj.*) thin
yasui *adj.* cheap (34)
yasumeru *v.t. II.* to give a rest
yasumi *n.* rest, vacation
yasumu *v.t. I.* to rest, to take a vacation
yattsu *numeral* eight (29)
yawarakai *adj.* soft, pliable
yen, en unit of money (35)
yo-dai four " units "
yogoreru *v.i. II.* to be soiled
yogoreta (*adj.*) soiled
yoi *adj.* good (5)
yo-ji four o'clock (35)
yokka four days, fourth day (36)
yoko *n.* side, width
yoko-no *n-adj.* sidewise, horizontal
yokogiru *v.t. I.* to cross over
yoku *n.* greed, desire
yokubaru *v.i. I.* to be greedy
yokubatta (*adj.*) greedy
yo-kumi four sets, four pairs (32)
yo-mai four sheets (32)

yomu *v.t. I.* to read (17)

yon-hai four (cup) fuls (32)

yon-hiki four " heads " (32)

yon-hon four " sticks " (32)

yon-satsu four volumes (32)

yon-sen four sen (35)

yoo *postp.* like, as

yoo *n.* work, business

yoofuku *n.* European style clothing

yooi *n.* preparation

yooi-suru *v.t. irr.* to prepare

yooka eight days, eighth day of the month (36)

yori *postp.* from, more—than (34)

yorokobi *n.* delight

yorokobu *v.t. I.* to be glad about

yoru *n.* night, evening

yo-sa *n.* goodness

yottari four persons (32)

yottsu *numeral* four (28)

yowai *adj.* weak

yo-yen four yen (35)

yu, o-yu *n.* hot water, bath

yubi *n.* finger

yubiwa *n.* ring

yuka *n.* floor (11)

yuki *n.* snow

yume *n.* dream

yunomi *n.* drinking cup (26)

yurumeru *v.t. II.* to loosen

yurumu *v.i. I.* to become loose

yurusu *v.t. I.* to forgive, to permit

yuubin *n.* mail, post

yuuki *n.* courage

Z

zabuton *n.* cushion (16)

zaimoku *n.* lumber

zaisan *n.* property

zankoku-na *n-adj.* cruel

zashiki *n.* parlour (16)

zatsu-na *n-adj.* miscellaneous, coarse

zei *n.* tax

zeitaku-na *n-adj.* extravagant

zettai-no *n-adj.* absolute

zoku-suru *v.i. irr.* to belong

zoo *n.* elephant

zoori *n.* sandals (39)

zubon *n.* trousers

zurui *adj.* crafty, unfair

zuuzuushii *adj.* shameless, impudent

English-Japanese Vocabulary

A

able, be dekiru *v.i. II.* (48);
-areru, -rareru *auxil. v.* (47)

about bakari, hodo *suf.*

absolute zettai-no *n-adj.*

accidental guuzen-no *n-adj.*

accountant, accounts kaikei *n.*

accustomed nareta (*adj.*)

accustomed, become nareru
v.i. II.

ache, to itamu *v.i. I.*

acid san *n.*

acquire, to toru *v.t. I.*, eru *v.t. II.*

add, to tsukeru *v.t. II.* soeru
v.t. II.

adjust, to choosetsu-suru *v.t.
irr.*

adjustment choosetsu *n.*

adrift, set nagasu *v.t. I.*

advance, to susumu *v.i. I.*

advertise, to kookoku-suru *v.
irr.*

advertisement kookoku *n.*

aeroplane hikooki *n.*

afternoon gogo, hiru-sugi *n.*

again mata *adv.*

age toshi *n.* nen *suf.*

agent dairi, daihyoo *n.*

ago mae *adv.* (35)

agriculture noogyoo *n.*

air kuuki *n.*

airplane hikooki *n.*

alcove tokonoma *n.* (16)

alive iki-te-iru (*adj.*)

all mina, subete *n.*, *n-adj.*

almost hotondo *adv.*

already moo (43), sude-ni *adv.*

also mo, mata *postp.*

always itsumo *adv.* (15)

among -de, -no naka-de, -no
naka-ni (34)

ancestor sosen, senzo *n.*

and to (4), te, ya *postp.*, soshite
con. (14)

anger ikari *n.*

angle kaku *n.*

angry, be okoru, ikaru *v.i. I.*

animal (living thing) doobutsu
iki-mono *n.*

another hoka-no, moo hitotsu
no *n-adj.* (49)

answer, to kotaeru *v.i. II.*

answer kotae, henji *n.*

ant ari *n.*

anxiety shinpai *n.*

anxious, be shinpai-suru *v.t. irr*

anything nandemo, nanika
not anything nanimo

apologize, to ayamaru *v.i. I.*

apparently rashii *adj.*

apple ringo *n.*

appropriate tekitoo-na *n-adj.*,
choodo-yoi *adj.*

approval sansei *n.*

approve, to sansei-suru *v.i. irr.*

April Shigatsu (36)

argue, to giron-suru *v.t. irr.*

argument giron, ron *n.*

arm ude *n.*

armament buki, busoo *n.*

army rikugun, guntai *n.*

arrange, to tehai-suru, tsugoo-suru, seiri-suru *v.t. irr.*

arrangement tehai, seiri *n.*

arrival toochaku *n.*

arrive, to tsuku *v.i. I.*

arrow ya *n.*

art gijutsu (technique), gei-jutsu, bijutsu (fine arts) *n*

as yoo-ni, hodo *postp.*

as far as made *postp.* (20)

ashamed, be hajiru *v.t. II*

ashes hai *n.*

at ni (9), de, nite *postp.*

at once sugu-ni *adv.* (47)

attach, to tsukeru *v.t. II.*

attack, to semeru *v.t. II.*, koo-geki-suru *v.t. irr.*

attack koogeki *n.*

attention chuui *n.*

attitude taido *n.*

audible, be kikoeru *v.i. II*

August Hachigatsu (36)

aunt oba *n.*

authority ken-i *n.*

automatic jidoo, jidoo-teki (*adj.*)

automobile jidoo-sha *n.* (52)

autumn aki *n.*

average heikin *n.*

average, to heikin-suru *v.t. irr.*

avoid, to sakeru *v.t. II.*

B

back ushiro (12), senaka *n.*

back side ura *n.,* ushiro *n.* (12)

bacteria baikin *n.*

bad warui *adj.* (5)

bag fukuro, kaban (suitcase) *n.*

ball tama, mari *n.*

bamboo take *n.*

bank ginkoo *n.*

bank (embankment) dote, tsu-tsumi *n.*

bank note satsu, shihei *n.*

banquet enkai *n.*

base dai *n.*

basement chikashitsu *n.*

basin tarai, senmenki *n.*

basis moto *n.*

basket kago *n.*

bath furo, yu *n.*

battle tatakai, sentoo *n.*

be, to aru *v.i. irr.* (41), iru *v.i. II.* (10), oru *v.i. I.*, gozai-masu

beans mame *n.*

bear, to (bring forth) umu *v.t. I.*

beautiful utsukushii *adj.*

beauty utsukushisa *n.*

because kara *con.* (47)

become, to naru *v.i. I.* (46, 54)

bed toko, shindai *n.*

bee hachi *n.*

beer biiru *n.*

before mae *adv.* (35)

beggar kojiki *n.*

begin, to hajimeru *v.t. II.* hajimaru *v.i. I.* (42)

beginning hajime *n.*

behind -no ushiro-ni (12)

believe, to shinjiru *v.t. II.*

belong, to zoku-suru, fuzoku-suru *v.i. irr.*

belt obi *n.*

bend, to mageru *v.t. II.*, magaru *v.i. I.*, oru *v.t. I.*, oreru *v.i. II.*

between naka (11), aida *n.*

bicycle jitensha *n.* (52)

big ookii *adj.* (5)

bind, to (as a book) tojiru *v.t. II.*

bird, tori *n.*

bite, to kamu *v.t. I.*

bitter nigai *adj.*

black kuro *n.*, kuroi *adj.*

blood chi *n.*

blow, to fuku *v.i. I.*

blue ao *n.*, aoi *adj.*

board ita *n.*

boat fune *n.*

body karada *n.*

boil, to niru *v.t. II.*, wakasu *v.t. I.*, waku *v.i. I.*

boiled rice gohan *n.* (22)

bolt (screw) neji *n.*

bone hone *n.*

book hon *n.* (1)

bookcase honbako *n.* (11)

border sakai *n.*

born, be umareru *v.i. II.*

borrow kariru *v.t. II.*

bottle bin *n.*

boundary sakai, kyookai *n.*

bow, to rei-suru, ojigi-suru *v.i. irr.*

bowl donburi, o-wan, chawan *n.*

box hako *n.* (4)

boy otoko-no ko (42), kodomo *n.*

brain noo *n.*

branch eda *n.*

brass shinchuu *n.*

bread pan *n.*

break, to kowasu (25, 49), oru (bend), waru (crack), yaburu (tear) *v.t. I.*

break, to kowareru, oreru (bend), wareru (crack), yabureru (tear) *v.i. II.*

breakfast asa-gohan (26), asa-meshi *n.*

breath iki *n.*

breathe, to iki-wo suru

brick renga *n.*

bridge hashi *n.*

bring, to motte-kuru *v.t. irr.* (24)

brush hake, fude (writing brush) *n.*

bucket baketsu, teoke *n.*

bud me, tsubomi (budding flower) *n.*

Buddha Hotoke-sama, Butsu

build, to tateru *v.t. II.*

bunch taba *n.*

bundle tsutsumi *n.*

burn, to yaku, moyasu *v.t. I*

burn, to yakeru, moeru *v.i. I.*

bury, to umeru, uzumeru *v.t. II.*

buried, become umaru uzumaru *v.i. I.*

business shigoto, yoo (work); torihiki (transaction) *n.*

busy isogashii *adj.* ⌜con.

but keredomo (14), shikashi

butterfly choocho *n.*

button botan *n.*

buy, to kau *v.t. I.* (21)

by de, motte *postp.*

by means of -de *postp.* (38)

C

cake kashi, o-kashi *n.*

calendar koyomi *n.*

call, to iu *v.i., v.t. I.* (38)

can -areru, -rareru, *auxil. v.* (47), dekiru *v.i. II.* (48)

can kan *n.*

cane tsue *n.*

car kuruma *n.*

card fuda, meishi (name card)

carp fish koi *n.*

carp streamer koi-nobori *n.* (46)

cash genkin *n.*

cat neko *n.*

catch, to toru *v.t. I.*, (23) tsuka-maeru *v.t. II*

cause gen-in *n.*

ceiling tenjoo *n.* (16)

cement semento *n.* (16)

center mannaka, chuuoo *n.*

certain (sure) tashika-na *n-adj*

certain aru (*adj.*)

chain kusari *n.*

chair isu *n.* (34)

chance kikai, ori *n.*

change, to kawaru *v.i. I.*, henka-suru *v.i. irr.*

change, to kaeru *v.t. II.*

change henka *n.*

chapter shoo *n.*

character seishitsu, seikaku *n.*

charcoal sumi *n.*

charge, take azukaru *v.t. I.*

charming kawaii *adj.*

cheap yasui *adj.* (34)

cheat, to gomakasu, damasu *v.t. I.*

chemical kusuri *n.*

chemistry kagaku *n.*

cherry sakura-no ki (tree), sakuranbo (fruit) *n.*

chest (breast) mune *n.*

chest of drawers tansu *n.*

chew, to kamu *v.t. I.*

chicken niwa-tori *n.*

child ko, kodomo *n.* (33, 42, 51)

china ware setomono, tooki *n.*

choose, to erabu, yoru *v.t. I.*

chop sticks hashi, o-hashi *n.* (26) ⌜*n.*

cinema eiga, katsudoo-shashin

circle maru, en, wa *n.*

city shi, machi *n.*

civilization bunka, bunmei *n.*

class kumi, kyuu, kaikyuu *n.*

claw tsume *n.*

clean kirei-na *n-adj.* (6)

clock tokei *n.*

clogg, to tsumeru *v.t. II.*

clogged, be tsumaru *v.i. I.*

close, to shimeru, tojiru *v.t. II.*

close, to shimaru *v.i. I.*, tojiru *v.i. II.*

closet todana *n.* (11)

cloth kire, nuno, *n.*

clothing kimono *n.* (4), yoofuku (European style)

cloud kumo *n.*

club (association) kurabu *n.*

clumsy bukiyoo-na, heta-na *n-adj.*

coal sekitan *n.*

coffee koohii *n.*

cold samui (weather), tsumetai (thing) *adj.*

coldness (degree of) samusa (weather), tsumetasa (thing)

colonization shokumin *n.* ⌊ *n.*

colonize, to shokumin-suru *v.t., v.i. irr.*

colour iro *n.*

comb kushi *n.*

come, to kuru *v.i. irr.* (19, 41)

come (command) koi

come out, to deru *v.i., v.t. II.*, de-te-kuru *v.i. irr.* (24)

comfortable kokochi-yoi *adj.*

company (corporation) kaisha *n.*

compare kuraberu *v.t. II.*, hikaku-suru *v.t. irr.*

comparison hikaku *n.*

complaint fuhei *n.*

compromise dakyoo *n.*

compromise, **to** dakyoo-suru *v.i. irr.*

concerning -ni tsuite

condition jootai, arisama *n.*

connect, to tsunagu *v.t. I.*

connection renraku *n.*

conscious, be ishiki-ga aru

consciousness ishiki *n.*

console, to nagusameru *v.t. II.*

consult, to soodan-suru *v.t. irr.*

consultation soodan *n.*

contact renraku *n.*, to contact renraku-suru *v.i. irr.*

contest kyoosoo *n.* to contest kyoosoo-suru *v.i. irr.*, arasou *v.t. I.*

continue, to tsuzukeru *v.t. II.* tsuzuku *v.i. I.*

convenience benri, tsugoo *n.*

convenient benri-na *n-adj.*, tsugoo-yoi *adj.*

cook ryoori-nin *n.*

cook, to ryoori-suru *v.t. irr.*

cooking ryoori, kappoo *n.*

cool suzushii *adj.*, coolness suzushisa *n.*

cool, to hiyasu *v.t. I.*

cool, become hieru *v.i. II.*

copper doo *n.*

corner kado, sumi *n.*

correct tadashii *adj.*

correct, to naosu *v.t. I.*

correct, become naoru *v.i. I.*

correspondence tsuushin *n.*

cost atai, hiyoo *n.*

cotton wata, momen *n.*

cough seki *n.*, to cough seki-suru *v.i. irr.*

count kanjoo *n.*

count, to kazoeru *v.t. II.* (52), kanjoo-suru *v.t. irr.*

counterfeit nise-no *n-adj.*

country (nation) kuni *n.*

countryside inaka *n.*

courage yuuki *n.*

cover futa *n.*

cow (ox) ushi *n.*

crafty zurui *adj.*

crazy kichigai-no *n-adj.*

crazy person kichigai *n.*

crease orime *n.*

crime tsumi *n.*

crooked magatta (*adj.*)

cross over, to yokogiru *v.t. I.*

crowd mure, gunshuu *n.*

cruel mugoi *adj.*, zankoku-na *n-adj.*

cry, to naku *v.i. I.*

culture bunka, kyooyoo (personal) *n.*

cupboard todana *n.* (11)

cushion zabuton *n.* (16)

custom fuuzoku, shuukan (habit) *n.*

cut, to kiru *v.t. I.*

D

damage gai, songai *n.*

damage, to kowasu *v.t. I.*, gai-suru *v.t. irr.*

dance odori *n.*

dance, to odoru *v.t. I.*

danger kiken *n.*

dangerous abunai *adj.*, kiken-na *n-adj.*

dark kurai *adj.*

day hi *n.*, nichi *suf.* (36)

day time hiru *n.*

December Juu-ni-gatsu (36)

decide, to kimeru *v.t. II.*

decided, become kimaru *v.i. I.*

decorate, to kazaru *v.t. I.*

decoration kazari *n.*

deep fukai *adj.*

defend, to mamoru *v.t. I.*, fuse-gu *v.t. I.*

delight yorokobi *n.*

deliver, to todokeru *v.t. II.*

deposite, to azukeru (entrust) *v.t. II.*, tameru (pile up) *v.t. II.*

depth fukasa *n.*

deputy dairi (agent) *n.*

desire nozomi, yoku *n.*

desire, to nozomu *v.t. I.*, hoshi-garu *v.t. I.*

desirous -tai (52), hoshii *adj.* (52)

desk tsukue *n.* (15)

detestable nikui, nikurashii *adj.*

device (mechanism) shikake *n.*

device, make shikakeru *v.t. II.*

devoted chuugi-na (for master), kookoo-na (for parents), chuujitsu-na (faithful in general) *n-adj.*

devotion chuugi (for master), kookoo (for parent), chuuji-tsusa (faithfulness in general) *n.*

dew tsuyu *n.*

dictionary jibiki, jisho *n.*

die, to shinu *v.i. I.* (54)

different chigau, chigatta (*adj.*

difficult muzukashii *adj.*, konnan-na *n-adj.*

difficulty muzukashisa, konnan *n.*

dig, to horu *v.t. I.*

dining room shokudoo *n.*

dining table chabu-dai *n.* (26)

diplomacy gaikoo *n.*

direct, to sashizu-suru, shihai-suru *v.t. irr.*

direction (command) shihai, sashizu; (line of course) hoogaku *n.*

dirty kitanai *adj.* (6)

disagreeable iya-na *n-adj.*

discourteous burei-na *n-adj.*

discover, to hakken-suru *v.t. irr.*, mitsukeru *v.t. II.*

discovery hakken *n.*

disease byooki *n.*

disgraced, be haji-wo kaku

dislike, to kirau *v.t. I.*

dissolve, to tokeru *v.i. II.*, tokasu *v.t. I.*

distance kyori, toosa *n.*

distinct hakkiri-shita (*adj.*)

do, to suru *v.t. irr.* (17, 41), yaru *v.t. I.*, itashi-masu

dog inu *n.* (10)

doll ningyoo *n.*

door to *n.* (28)

doubt utagai *n.*

doubt, to utagau *v.t. I.*

drama shibai, geki *n.*

drawer hikidashi *n.* (33)

dream yume *n.*

dream, to yume-wo miru

dress kimono *n.* (4)

drink, to nomu *v.t. I.*

drinking cup yunomi *n.*

drip, to tareru *v.i. II.*

drip, let (to spill) tarasu *v.t. I.*

drop shizuku *n.*

dry kawaita (*adj.*)

dry, to kawakasu *v.t. I.*

dry, to kawaku *v.i. I.*

dull tsumaranai(uninteresting) *adj.*, nibui (slow, dull) *adj.*

dust chiri, hokori *n.*

duty gimu *n.*

dwelling sumai *n.*, to dwell sumau *v.i. I.*

E

ear mimi *n.*

early hayai *adj.*

earnest majime-na *n-adj.*

earth chikyuu (the globe) tsuchi (ground) *n.*

earthquake jishin *n.*

east higashi *n.*

easy yasashii *adj.*, raku-na *n-adj.*

eat, to taberu *v.t. II.*, kuu *v.t. I.*

economy, economics keizai *n.*

edge heri *n.*, edge of a knife ha *n.* ⌈*irr.*

educate, to kyooiku-suru *v.t.*

education kyooiku *n.*

egg tamago *n.*

eight yattsu, hachi *n-adj.* (29, 30); — **days** yooka, — **pairs**, — **sets** yakumi (32)

elder brother ani *n.*

elder sister ane *n.*

election senkyo *n.*, **to elect** senkyo-suru *v.t. irr.*

electricity denki *n.* ⌈*n.* (16)

electric car (street car) densha

electric light dentoo (16)

elephant zoo *n.*

eleven juu-ichi *n-adj.* (30); — **minutes** juu-ippun, — **volumes** juu-issatsu (32)

eliminate, to habuku *v.t. I.*

emergency hijoo *n.*

Emperor Kootei *n.*, **Japanese Emperor** Tennoo *n.*

Empire Teikoku *n.* (54)

employ, to tsukau *v.t. I.* (37)

Empress Jo-oo *n.*; **Japanese Empress** Koozoo *n.*

empty kara-na, kara-no *n-adj.*

enclosure kakoi *n.*

encourage, to susumeru *v.t. II.*, shoorei-suru *v.t. irr.*

end owari, oshimai *n.*

end, to owaru *v.i. I.*, oshimai-ni naru

English language Ei-go *n.* (38)

enjoy, to tanoshimu *v.t. I.*

enough juubun *n-adj.*

enter, to hairu *v.i. v.t. I.* (39)

entirely mina, subete (*adv.*)

entrance iri-guchi, kuchi *n.*

entrance hall genkan *n.* (39)

etiquette reigi *n.*

Europe Yooroppa, Seiyoo

European Seiyoo-no *n-adj.*, Seiyoo-jin (people) *n.*

even sae *postp.*

evening ban *n.*

every mai *pref.*, goto-ni *suf.*

examine, to mi-te-miru *v.t. II.* (24), shiraberu *v.t. II.*

example rei *n.*

excell, to sugureru *v.i. II.*

excellent sugureta (*adj*)

excite, to shigeki-suru *v.t. irr.*

excited, be sawagu *v.t. I.*

exercise (physical) undoo *n.*

exercise, to undoo-suru *v.i. irr.*

expensive takai *adj.* 13, 34)

experience keiken *n.* ⌈*irr.*

experience, to keiken-suru *v.t.*

explain, to setsumei-suru *v.t. irr.*

explanation setsumei *n.*

explode, to bakuhatsu-suru, haretsu-suru *v.i. irr.*

explosion bakuhatsu, haretsu *n.*

eye me *n.*

F

fabric ori-mono *n.*

face (countenance) kao *n.*

fact koto, jissai (reality) *n.*

factory koojoo *n.*

fail, to shippai-suru *v.i. irr.*

failure shippai *n.*

faint (dim) kasuka-na *n-adj.*

faint, to kizetsu-suru *v.i. irr.*

faithful chuujitsu-na, chuugi-na (to master), kookoo-na (to parents) *n-adj.*

fall, to chiru (scatter) *v.i. I.*, furu (rain) *v.i. I.*, ochiru (drop down) *v.i. II.*, taoreru (topple over) *v.i. II.*

familiar shitashii *adj.*

family uchi (home), katei (family circle) *n.*

far tooi *adj.* (51)

far as, as made *postp.*

farm noojoo *n.*

farmer hyakushoo, noofu *n.*

fashion ryuukoo *n.*

fat abura *n.*

fat futotta (*adj.*)

fat, grow futoru *v.i. I.*

father chichi, otoo-san *n.*

fatigue tsukare *n.*

fear osore *n.*

fear, to osoreru *v.t. II.*

fearful osoroshii, kowai *adj.*

feast go-chisoo *n.*

feather hane *n.*

February Nigatsu (36)

feel, to kanjiru *v.t. II.*

feeling kanji *n.*

female mesu *n. & n-adj.*

fence kakoi, kakine *n.*

festival matsuri, o-matsuri *n.* (46)

fever netsu *n.*

few wazuka-na, sukoshi-no *n-adj.* (44)   ⌈field⌉ *n.*

field nohara, hatake (farm

fifth day itsukame ; fifth day of the month itsuka

fight tatakai, kenka *n.*

fight, to tatakau *v.i. I.*

filial devotion kookoo *n.*

fill, to mitasu *v.t. I.*, ippai-ni suru

fine rippa-na (magnificent) *n-adj.* (7), komakai (small) *adj.*

fine arts geijutsu, bijutsu *n.*

fine weather hare *n.*, yoi tenki

finger yubi *n.*

finish, to sumu *v.i. I.*

finish, to shimau *v.t. I.*

fire hi *n.*

fire (house on fire) kaji *n.*

fire brazier hibachi *n.* (15)

first day of the month Tsuita-chi (36)

first year of an era Gan-nen (36)

fish sakana *n.* (46), uo *n.*

five itsutsu (29), go (30) *n-adj.* ; five days itsuka, five pairs. five sets itsu-kumi (32)

flag hata *n.*

flame honoo *n.*

flat taira-na *n-adj.* (6)

flea nomi *n.*

flee, to nigeru *v.i. II.*

floor yuka *n.*

floor (storey) kai *suf.* (52)

flow, to nagareru *v.i. II.*

flower hana *n.*   ⌈(26)

flower arrangement ikebana *n.*

flower vase kabin *n.* (16)

fly, to tobu *v.i.* I.

fly (insect) hai, hae *n.*

fog kiri *n.*

fold, to oru *v.t.* I.

fond of, be suku *v.t.I.*, suki *n-adj.* (52)

fool baka *n.*, *interj.*

foot ashi *n.*

foreign country gaikoku *n.*

forget, to wasureru *v.t.* II. (25)

forgive me, please gomen-nasai

four yottsu (28), shi (30) *n-adj.*;
— days yokka, — o'clock yo-ji, — persons yottari, — sheets yo-mai, — sen yon-sen, — yen yon-yen, — volumes yon-satsu (32)

frame waku, fuchi *n.*

free jiyuu-na *n-adj.*

free of charge tada-no *n-adj.*

freeze, to kooru *v.i.* I.

friction masatsu *n.*

Friday Kin-yoobi *n.* (36)

friend tomo-dachi *n.*, good friends nakayoshi *n.*

from yori (19, 34), kara *postp.*

front mae *n.*, in front of -no mae-ni (12)

frontispiece kuchi-e *n.* (42)

fruit kudamono, mi *n.*

-ful hai *suf.* (31)

full ippai *n-adj.*

full, become michiru *v.i.* II., ippai-ni naru

furniture kagu, doogu *n.*

future mirai *n.*

G

garden niwa *n.* (10)

gas gasu *n.*

gate mon *n.*

gather, to atsumaru *v.i.* I.

gather, to atsumeru *v.t.* II.

gathering atsumari *n.*

gay hade-na, nigiyaka-na *n-adj.*

genteel joohin-na *n-adj.*

geography chiri *n.*

get up, to okiru *v.i.* II.

girl onna-no ko *n.* (42)

give, to ageru (send up) *v.t.* II., (27) yaru (to inferior person) *v.t.* I., ataeru *v.t.* II.

give, to kudasaru (send down) *v.t.* I. (27)

give up, to yameru (to stop), akirameru (to lose hope) *v.t.* II.

glad, be yorokobu *v.t.* I.

glass garasu, koppu (drinking glass) *n.*

go, to iku *v.i.* I.

god kami, kami-sama *n.*

gold kin *n.*

good yoi, ii *adj.* (5)

goodbye sayonara (39)

good friend nakayoshi *n.*, *n-adj.* (42)

goodness yosa *n.*

go on foot, to aruite-iku *v.i.*, *v.t.* I. (24)

go out, to deru *v.i.*, *v.t. II.* (24), de-te-iku (24)

go over, to (to cross) koeru *v.t. II.*, kosu *v.t. I.*

go up, to agaru, noboru *v.t. I.*

government seifu *n.*

government office yakusho, ya-kuba *n.*

grade kyuu (class), saka (hill) *n.*

grain tsubu (particle), kokumo-tsu (cereals) *n.*

grand ookii *adj.*, rippa-na *n-adj.*

grandfather ojii-san, sofu *n.*

grandmother obaa-san, sobo *n.*

grapes budoo *n.*

grass kusa *n.*

gratis tada, muryoo *n-adj.*

gratitude kansha *n.*

grave haka ; grave yard haka-ba, bochi *n.*

gravel jari *n.*

greed yoku *n.*

greedy yokubatta (*adj.*)

green midori-no *n-adj.*

greet, to aisatsu-suru *v.i. irr.*

greeting aisatsu, rei *n.*

grieve, to kanashimu *v.t. I.*

grund jimen *n.*

group dantai *n.*

grow, to nobiru *v.i. II.*, naru *v.i. I.* (46) ookiku naru

guard bannin *n.*

guard, to stand ban-suru *v.t. irr.*

guest kyaku, o-kyaku *n.* (16, 39)

guidance shidoo *n.*

guide annai *n.*

guide, to annai-suru *v.t. irr.*

gun teppoo *n.*

H

hair ke, kami (hair of the head) *n.*

half han (35), hanbun *n.*

half past han, han sugi (35)

hand te *n.*

handle e *n.*

hang, to kakaru *v.i. I.*

hang, to kakeru *v.t. II.*

hanging scroll kakemono *n.* (16)

happiness koofuku, saiwai *n.*

happy koofuku-na, saiwai-na *n-adj.*, medetai (worthy of congratulation) *adj.*

harbour minato *n.*

hard katai *adj.*

hardness katasa *n.*

hardship kurushimi *n.*

harm gai *n.*

harmonize, to choowa-suru *v.i. rr.*

harmony choowa *n.*

hat booshi *n.*

hate, to nikumu *v.t. I.*

have, to motsu *v.t. I.* (18)

have been to, to itte-kuru *v.i. irr.* (24)

he sono hito, kare *pron.*

head atama, kashira (head man) *n.*

health kenkoo *n.*

hear, to kiku *v.t. I.*

heart shinzoo, kokoro (mind) *n*.

heat netsu, atsusa *n*.

heavy omoi *adj*.

height takasa *n*.

Hello (a call) moshi moshi

help tasuke, tetsudai *n*.

help, to tasukeru *v.t. II*., tetsu-dau *v.t. I*.

hemp asa *n*.

here koko *pron*. (9)

hide, to kakusu *v.t. I*., kakure-ru *v.i. II*.

high takai *adj*. (13, 34)

hill saka (slope), yama, oka (high ground) *n*.

hinge chootsugai *n*.

hip koshi *n*.

history rekishi *n*.

hoe kuwa *n*.

hold, to motsu *v.t. I*. (18) nigiru *v.t. I*.

hole ana *n*.

holiday yasumi (vacation), sai-jitsu (flag day) *n*.

home uchi *n*. (14)

honest shoojiki-na *n-adj*., tada-shii *adj*.

hope nozomi *n*.

hope, to nozomu *v.t. I*.

horizontal suihei-na, yoko-no *n-adj*.

horn tsuno, fue (trumpet) *n*.

horse uma *n*.

hospital byooin *n*.

host shujin *n*. ⌈*adj*.

hot atsui *adj*., karai (peppery)

hot water yu, o-yu *n*.

hotel yadoya, hoteru (foreign style) *n*.

hour jikan *n*. (35)

house uchi, ie *n*. (14)

house to let kashiya *n*.

however shikashi, keredomo (but) *con*.; ikani, donna-ni (as however much) *adv*.

how many ? ikutsu *n-adj*. (29) iku-*pref*.

how many days ? iku-nichi, nan-nichi ; how many weeks ? iku-shuukan, nan-shuukan ; how many months ? nan-ka-getsu (36) ; how many (cup) fuls ? nan-bai ; how many "heads" ? nan-biki ; how many "sticks" ? nan-bon (32)

how much ? ikura (35) dono-kurai *n-adj*., iku *pref*.

human being ningen *n*.

hundred hyaku *n-adj*.

hurry, to isogu *v.t. I*. ⌈*n*.

hydrant (water tap) suidoo-sen

I

I watakushi (1), watashi, boku (used by young men), ore (used by men), jibun (formal) *pron*.

ice koori *n*.

idea kangae *n*.

if moshimo...naraba, moshimo ...kereba (53)

imagination soozoo *n.*

immediately sugu-ni *adv.*

Imperial Teikoku *n-adj.*

Imperial University Teikoku Daigaku *n.* (54)

imply, to fukumu *v.t. I.*

important taisetsu-na *n-adj.* (6)

impudent zuuzuushii, *adj.*

impure niggota (*adj.*) fujun-na *n-adj.*

impurity nigori, fujun-butsu *n.*

in ni (9, 11), de (34) *postp.*, -no. naka-ni (11), -no naka de (34)

industry koogyoo *n.*

inexpensive yasui *adj.* (34)

inferior ototta, yoku-nai (*adj.*)

influence eikyoo *n.*

influence, to eikyoo-suru *v.i. irr.*

injure, to itameru, kizutsukeru *v.t. II.*

injury kizu, kega *n.*

ink sumi, inku, inki *n.*

inn yadoya *n.*

inquire, to tou *v.t. I.*, tazuneru *v.t. II.*

insane kichigai-no *n-adj.*, kichigai (insane person) *n.*

insect mushi *n.* (10)

inside naka (11) uchi *n.*

insurance hoken *n.*

insure, to hoken-wo tsukeru

intelligence chie, chinoo *n.*

intelligent rikoo-na *n-adj.* (13) kashikoi *adj.*

intend, to kokorozasu *v.t. I.*

intention kokorozashi, kangae *n.*

interest kyoomi (amusement), rishi (profit) *n.*

interesting omoshiroi *adj.* (51) kyoomi-no aru

international kokusai, kokusai-teki *n-adj.*

interrupt, to jama-suru *v.t. irr.*

interruption jama *n.*

intimate shitashii *adj.*

introduce, to shookai-suru *v.t. irr.*

introduction shookai *n.*

invent, to hatsumei-suru *v.t. irr.*

invention hatsumei *n.*

invitation shootai, maneki *n.*

invite, to maneku *v.t. I.*, shootai-suru *v.t. irr.*

iron tetsu, hinoshi (flat iron) *n.*

iron, to hinoshi-wo kakeru

it sore, are *pron.*; its sono, sore-no, ano, are-no (*adj.*)

itchy kayui, kaii *adj.*

J

January Ichigatsu (36)

Japan Nippon, Nihon (15)

Japanese Nippon-no, Nihon-no *n-adj.* (15); Nippon-jin, Nihon-jin (Japanese person) *n.*

jar tsubo *n.*

jaw ago *n.*

joke joodan *n.*

judge saiban-kan *n.*

judge, to saiban-suru (to sit in judgement), handan-suru (to consider) *v.t. irr.*

judgement saiban, handan *n.*

juice shiru, tsuyu *n.*

July Shichigatsu (36)

jump, to tobu *v.i. I.*, haneru *v.i. II.*

June Rokugatsu (36)

K

keep, to totte-oku (as keep a thing), mamoru (as keep a law) *v.t. I.*

kerosene sekiyu *n.*

kettle kama, yakan, nabe *n.*

key kagi *n.*

kick, to keru *v.t. I.*

kill, to korosu *v.t. I.*

kind (sort) rui *n.*

kindness shinsetsu *n.*, kind shinsetsu-na *n-adj.* (13)

King Oo, Oo-sama, *n.*

knee hiza *n.*

knot musubime (tie), kobu (hump) *n.*

know, to shiru *v.t. I.*

knowledge chishiki *n.*

L

lacquer bowl o-wan *n.* (26)

ladder hashigo *n.*

land riku, chi *n.*

land, to jooriku-suru (from water), chakuriku-suru (from air) *v.i. irr.*

language kotoba *n.*, -go *suf.*

last owari-no, oshimai-no *n-adj.*, sen- *pref.*; last day of the month misoka; last month sen-getsu; last week sen-shuu; last year kyo-nen, saku-nen (36)

late osoi *adj.*

later (future) nochi-ni *adv.* (52

laugh, to warau *v.t. I.*

laundry sentaku *n.*; to wash sentaku-suru *v.t. irr.*

law hooritsu *n.*

laxative gezai *n.*

lead, to shidoo-suru *v.t. irr.*, michibiku *v.t. I.*

leader shidoo-sha *n.*

leaf (of a plant) ha *n.*

league renmei *n.*

learn, to oboeru *v.t. II.* (40)

learning gakumon *n.*

left hidari *n. & n-adj.* (12)

leg ashi *n.*

leisure hima *n.*

lend, to kasu *v.t. I.*

length nagasa *n.*

lengthwise tate-no *n-adj.*

let, to (a house) kasu *v.t. I.*

let, to -aseru, -saseru *auxil. v.* (50); to let someone do saseru *v.t. II.* (50)

let us -mashoo (21)

letter (ideograph) ji, kana *n.*

letter (communication) tegami *n.* (23, 38)

liberty jiyuu *n.*

library toshokan (building), to-shoshitsu (room) n.

lid futa n. (4)

lie uso, itsuwari n.

lie, to (to deceive) itsuwaru v.t. I., uso-wo tsuku

lie, to (to lie down) neru v.i. II.

life inochi; seikatsu (livelihood)n.

light hikari, akari n.

light (as against dark) akarui adj.

light in colour usui adj.

light in weight karui adj.

like yoo-na n-adj.

like, to konomu v.t. I., -ga suki-de su (52)

limit kagiri, gendo n.

limit, to kagiru v.t. I

line sen, suji n.; straight line choku sen

linen asa n.

lip kuchibiru n.

liquid eki n.

liquor sake n.

list hyoo n.

litre (unit of measure) rittoru

little (quantity sukoshi-no (44) wazuka-no n-adj.

live, to ikiru (to be alive) v.i. II. sumu (dwell) v.i. I., seikatsu suru (to make a living) v.i. irr.

lock joomae n.

long nagai adj. (54)

loosen, to yurumeru v.t. II. toku v.t. I

loosen, to yurumu v.i. I., toke ru v.i. II.,

love ai n.

love, to ai-suru v.t. irr.

loveliness airashisa n.

lovely airashii adj.

low hikui adj. (34)

lower part (under side) shita n

loyal chuugi-na (to master), chuujitsu-na n-adj.

loyalty chuugi (to master), chuujitsu n.

lucky medetai adj., un-no yoi

lumber zaimoku n.

lung hai n.

M

machine kikai n.

mad kichigai n-adj.; mad man kichigai n.

magnificent rippa-na n-adj. (7)

maid servant jochuu n.

mail yuubin n.

Majesty, his or her Heika suf. & n.

make, to tsukuru v.t. I. (25, 49), koshiraeru v.t. II.

male osu n. & n-adj.

man otoko (1), hito (person) (10), ningen (human being) n

manage, to shihai-suru, shori-suru v.t. irr., atsukau v.t. I.

management shihai, atsukai n.

manager shihai-nin n.

many takusan-no (29), ooku-no n-adj., ooi adj.

March Sangatsu (36)

mark shirushi, ten *n*.

marriage kekkon, konrei (ceremony) *n*.

marry, to kekkon-suru *v.i. irr*.

master shujin *n*.

matted floor tatami *n*.

matter koto, mono *n*.

May Go-gatsu (36)

meal go-han (22), meshi *n*.

mean, to imi-suru *v.t. irr*.

meaning imi *n*.

means of, by de, *postp*. -wo

measure masu, hakari *n*.

measure, to hakaru *v.t. I*.

meat niku *n*. (23)

medical art ijutsu *n*.

medicine (chemical) kusuri *n*.

meet, to au, atsumaru *v.i. I*.

meeting kai, atsumari *n*.

melt, to tokeru *v.i. II*., tokasu *v.t. I*., toku *v.t. I*.

memorial kinen *n*. (54)

memorize, to oboeru *v.t. II*., anki-suru *v.t. irr*.

memory kioku, oboe *n*.

messenger tsukai *n*. (37).

metal kane, kinzoku *n*.

meter meetaa, meetoru *n*.

method hoohoo, shikata, yari-kata *n*.

metre (unit of length) meetaa, meetoru

middle mannaka, chuuoo *n*.

Middle School Chuugakkoo *n*. (54)

mind kokoro *n*.

mineral matter koo-butsu *n*.

minute (unit of time) fun *n*.

mirror kagami *n*. (35)

mist kiri *n*.

mistake ayamari, machigai *n*.

mistake, to ayamaru *v.t. I*., machigaeru *v.t. II*.

mistaken machigatta (*adj*.)

mistress of a house okusan *n*. (39)

mix, to mazaru *v.i. I*., mazeru *v.t. II*.

modest otonashii *adj*., kenson-na *n-adj*.

moist shimetta, nureta (*adj*.)

moist, become shimeru *v.i. I*. nureru *v.i. II*.

moisten, to nurasu *v.t. I*.

Monday Getsuyoobi (36)

money kane, o-kane, kinsen *n*.

month tsuki *n*., gatsu *suf*., getsu *suf*. (36)

moon tsuki *n*. (36)

more motto, moo *adv*. (34)

morning asa, gozen (forenoon) *n*.

mosquito ka *n*.

moss koke *n*.

mother haha, o-kaa-san *n*.

motion undoo, ugoki *n*.

motion picture katsudoo-sha-shin, eiga *n*.

motor car jidoosha *n*. (52)

mountain yama *n*.

mouse nezumi *n*.

mouth kuchi *n.*

move, to ugoku *v.i. I.,* hikkosu (move one's residence) *v.t. I.*

movie katsudoo-shasin, eiga *n.*

Mr., Mrs., Miss., -san *suf.* (3)

much takusan-no *n-adj.*

muddiness nigori *n.* (29)

muddy niggota (*adj.*)

muddy, become nigoru *v.i. I.*

muddy, make nigosu *v.t. I.*

museum hakubutsu-kan *n.*

music ongaku *n.*

must -nakereba naranai, must not -tewa naranai (53)

mutual soogo, tagai-no *n-adj.*

N

nail kugi ; finger nail tsume *n.*

name namae, na *n.* (54)

narrow semai *adj.* (7)

nation kuni *n.*

nature (quality) tachi, seishitsu

nature (the great nature) shizen *n.*

navy kaigun *n.*

near chikai *adj.* (51)

necessary hitsuyoo-na *n-adj.*

necessity hitsuyoo *n.*

neck kubi *n.*

need, to iru *v.i. I.* (27), hitsuyoo to suru

needle hari *n.*

neighbourhood kinjo *n.*

neighbouring tonari-no (46), chikaku-no, kinjo-no *n-adj.*

nerve shinkei (nervous system) ;

dokyoo (courage) *n.*

net ami *n.*

new atarashii *adj.*

newness atarashisa *n.*

newspaper shinbun *n.* (17)

New Year's Day Ganjitsu (36)

next tsugi-no *n-adj.*

next door tonari *n.* (46)

next month rai-getsu (36)

next week rai-shuu (36)

next year rai-nen, myoo-nen

night yoru *n.* ⌊(36)

nine kokonotsu, ku, kyuu *n* (29, 30)

nine days kokonoka (36)

ninth day kokonoka (36)

no iie *interj.* (3)

no good dame *n-adj. & interj.*

noise oto, zatsu-on *n.*

noon o-hiru, shoogo *n.*

north kita *n.*

nose hana *n.*

not nai, nu *auxil. v., adv* (13, 51)

not anything, nothing nani-mo *adv.* (27)

note nooto *n.*

not one, not any hitotsu-mo *adv.* (28)

not yet mada *adv.* (43)

notify shiraseru *v.t. II.*

novel shoosetsu, hanashi *n.*

November Juu-ichi-gatsu (36)

now ima *n., adv.* (20)

nude hadaka-no *n-adj.*

number kazu, suu *n.*

number (ordinal) bangoo *n.*
(33), dai *pref.*, ban *suf.*, banme *suf.* (33)
nut (fruit) mi *n.*
nut (screw) neji, meneji *n.*

O

obey, to shitagau *v.i. I.*
object (purpose) mokuteki *n.*
object, to hantai-suru *v.i. irr.*
iyagaru *v.t. I.*
obligation giri *n.*
obstinate shitsukkoi *adj.*
obstruct, to samatageru *v.t. II.*,
jama-suru *v.t. irr.*
obstruction jama, samatage *n.*
o'clock ji *suf.* (35)
October Juugatsu (36)
of no *postp.* (4)
office jimusho (room) (52);
yaku (position) *n.*
officer, military shookoo *n.*
oil abura *n.*
old (antiquated) furui *adj.*
old (person) toshi-totta (*adj.*)
old man ojii-san ; old woman
obaa-san ; old person toshi-
yori *n.* ⌈(11)
on ni (9), de *postp.*, -no ue-ni
one hitotsu, ichi, *n-adj.* (27, 30);
— (cup) ful ippai, — "head"
ippiki, — minute ippun,
— person hitori, — sen issen,
— set, — pair hito-kumi,
— "stick" ippon, — volume
issatsu (32, 35)

one more moo hitotsu (49)
onion negi *n.*
only tada, tatta, *adv.*
open aita, hiraita (*adj.*)
open, to akeru *v.t. II.* (17), hiraku *v.t.I.*
open, to aku *v.i. I.* hiraku *v.i. I.*
operation (medical) shujutsu *n.*
oppose, to hantai-suru *v.i. irr.*
opposite hantai-no *n-adj.*
opposition hantai *n.*
order chuumon *n.*
order (command) meirei *n.* ⌈*n.*
order (sequence) junjo, junban
order, to chuumon-suru *v.t.*
irr. ; meirei-suru (to command) *v.t. irr.*
order that, in tame-ni (54)
order, to put in katazukeru *v.t.*
ordinary futsuu-no *n-adj.* ⌊*II.*
origin moto *n.*
ornament (to be set on tokonoma) oki-mono *n.* (16)
other hoka-no (53), ta-no *n-adj.*
outdoors soto, omote *n.*
outside soto, omote *n.*
overcoat gaitoo *n.*
over-garment haori *n.*
overthrow, to taosu *v.t. I.*

P

paddy field ta *n.*
page peiji *n. suf.*
pain itami *n.*
painful itai (sore), kurushii
(hard) *adj.*

paint penki, enogu *n*.

pair kumi (32), tsui *n*. & *suf*.

pan nabe *n*.

paper kami *n*. (31)

paper door fusuma (heavy) (16), shooji (light) *n*. (15)

paper money satsu *n*.

parallel heikoo-no *n-adj*.

parlour zashiki *n*. (16)

part bubun *n*.

part, to wakareru, hanareru *v.i. II*.

pass, to tooru *v.t. I*.; sugiru *v.t. II*.

past kako, mukashi *n*.

past sugi *suf*. (35)

paste nori *n*.

pay, to harau *v.t. I*.

pea mame *n*.

peace heiwa *n*.

peel, to muku, hagu *v.t. I*.

pencil enpitsu *n*. (8)

percentage wariai, buai *n*

perfect kanzen-na *n-adj*.

perfection kanzen *n*.

permit kyoka, yurushi *n*.

permit, to yurusu *v.t. I*.

person hito (10), mono *n*.

phonograph chikuonki *n*.

photograph shashin *n*. (46)

physician isha *n*.

physics butsuri-gaku *n*.

picture e *n*. (39)

piece kire, hen, ko *n*. & *suf*.

pig buta *n*.

pile up, to kasaneru, tsumi

ageru *v.t. II*.

pillar hashira *n*.

pine tree matsu *n*.

place tokoro (39), basho *n*.

place, to oku *v.t. I*. (46)

plan keikaku *n*.

plan, to keikaku-suru *v.t. irr*.

plant (plant life) shokubutsu *n*.

play (game) asobi *n*.

play, to (to have a good time asobu *v.i. I*. (42)

play ground undoojoo *n*.

please doozo *adv*. & *interj*. (28)

pleased, be yorokobu *v.t. I*.

pleasure (recreation) tanoshi-mi *n*.

pocket pokketto *n*.

poem uta, shi *n*.

point ten *n*.

poison doku *n*.

police keisatsu *n*.

police man junsa *n*.

polish, to migaku *v.t. I*.

polished migaita (*adj*.)

politics seiji *n*.

poor (destitute) binboo-na *n-adj*.

porcelain jiki *n*.

port minato *n*.

position ichi *n*., tokoro *n*. (39)

possible, to be -areru, -rareru *auxil. v*. (47), dekiru *v.i. II*. (48)

post yuubin *n*.

postage stamp kitte *n*.

post box yuubin-bako *n*.

post card hagaki *n*.

potato imo *n.*

powder kona *n.*

praise, to homeru *v.t. II.*

pray, to inoru *v.t. I.*

precious daiji-na, taisetsu-na *n-adj.* (6)

precision seimitsu *n.*

prefecture ken *n.*

preparation yooi, shitaku *n.*

prepare, to yooi-suru, shitaku-suru *v.t. irr.*

pretty kirei-na *n-adj.* (6), utsu-kushii *adj.*

price atai, nedan *n.*

pride hokori, jiman *n.*

Prince, Princess Miya-sama *n.*

print, to insatsu-suru *v.t. irr.*

printing insatsu *n.*

profit, rieki, toku *n.*

proof shooko ; koosei (of print-ing) *n.*

property zaisan *n.*

public ooyake-no *n-adj.*

pull, to hiku, hipparu *v.t. I.*

pump ponpu *n.*

punish, to bassuru *v.t. irr.*

punishment batsu *n.*

purple murasaki-no *n-adj.*

purpose mokuteki *n.*

push, to osu *v.t. I.*

push through, to toosu, oshi-toosu *v.t. I.*

put to (to place) oku *v.t. I.*

put away, to katazukeru *v.t. II.*

put in, to ireru *v.t. II.* ⌈*v.t. II.*

put in order, to katazukeru

put out, to dasu *v.t. I.*

put together, to awaseru *v.t. II.* tsunagu (connect) *v.t. I.*

Q

quality shitsu, gara, tachi *n.*

quantity bunryoo *n.*

quarrel arasoi, kenka *n.*

quarrel, to arasou *v.t. I.*, ken-ka-suru *v.i. irr.*

Queen Jooo *n.*

question toi, mondai *n.*

quick hayai *adj.*

quiet shizuka-na *n-adj.*, otona-shii *adj.* ⌈kari *adv.*

quite (entirely) mattaku, suk-

R

radio rajio *n.*

rail senro *n.*

railway tetsudoo *n.*

rain ame *n.*

rain, to furu *v.i. I.*

raise, to ageru *v.t. II.* (27, 46), okosu *v.t. I.*

rank retsu (column), kurai (position) *n.*

rat nezumi *n.*

rate wariai, buai *n.*

reach, to tsuku, todoku *v.i. I.*

read, to yomu *v.t. I.* (17)

real hontoo-no, jissai-no *n-adj.*

reason wake, rikutsu *n.*

receive, to ukeru *v.t. II.*, uke-toru *v.t. I.*, morau *v.t. I.*, ita-daku *v.t. I.*

recommend, to susumeru *v.t.* *II.*, suisen-suru *v.t. irr.*

recommendation suisen *n.*

record kiroku *n.*

record, to kiroku-suru *v.t. irr.*

recover, to naoru *v.i. I.*, kaifuku-suru *v.i. irr.*

recreation nagusami, tanoshimi *n.*

red aka *n.* akai *adj.*

reed mat tatami *n.* (15)

regret kuyami (condolence) *n.*

regret, to kuyamu *v.t. I.*

regulation kisoku, kimari, sadame *n.*

relation kankei, shinrui (blood relation) *n.*

religion shuukyoo *n.*

remain, to nokoru, amaru *v.i. I.*

remainder nokori, amari *n.*

remember, to oboeru *v.t. II.* (40)

repeat, to kurikaesu *v.t. I.*

report shirase, hookoku *n.*

report, to shiraseru *v.t. II.*, hookoku-suru *v.t. irr.*

represent, to daihyoo-suru *v.t. irr.*

representative daihyoo *n.*

request tanomi, negai *n.*

request, to tanomu, negau *v.t. I.*

resemble, to niru *v.i. II.*

reserve yobi-no *n-adj.* ; enryo (modesty) *n.*

respect sonkei *n.*

respect, to sonkei-suru *v.t. irr.*,

tootobu *v.t. I.*

responsibility sekinin *n.*

rest yasumi (repose), nokori (remainder) *n.*

rest, to yasumu *v.t. I.*, yasumaseru *v.t. II.*

result kekka *n.*

return kaeri (way back), rieki (profit) *n.*

return, to kaeru *v.i. I.*

reverse sakasama (upside down), ushiro-muki (backward) *n. & n-adj.*

revise, to aratameru, kaeru *v.t. II.*

reward mukui, hooshuu *n.*

rice kome (grain), gohan (boiled rice) *n.*

rice bowl chawan *n.* (26)

rice tub o-hitsu *n.* (26)

rich kanemochi-no *n-adj.* tonda (*adj.*)

ride, to noru *v.i. I.* (21)

right (claim) kenri *n.*

right (honest) tadashii *adj.*

right migi *n.*, *n-adj.* (12) [*n.*

ring wa, yubi-wa (finger ring

rise, to okiru (get up) *v.i. II* agaru (go up) *v.i. I.*

river kawa *n.*

rivet byoo *n.*

road michi, dooro *n.*

roll, to korogasu *v.t. I.*, korogaru *v.i. I.*, maku (to wind) *v.t.*

roof yane *n.* [*I.*

room heya (7) shitsu *n.*

root ne, nemoto *n.*

rope nawa, himo *n.*

rose bara *n.*

rot, to kusaru *v.i. I.*

rough arai *adj.*

round marui *adj.*

rub, to suru, kosuru *v.t. I.*

rule kisoku *n.*

rule, to shihai-suru *v.t. irr.*

ruler shihai-sha *n.*; joogi, monosashi (instrument) *n.*

run, to hashiru *v.i. I.* (42), kakeru *v.i. II.*

run away, to nigeru *v.i. II.*

rust sabi *n.*

rust, to sabiru *v.i. II.*

S

sad kanashii *adj.*

safe anzen-na, daijoobu-na *n-adj.*

safe (a vault) kinko *n.*

safety anzen, buji *n.*

sail ho *n.*

sail, to (to start) shuppan-suru *v.i. irr.*

sake of, for the tame-ni

salt shio *n.*

salty karai, shio-karai *adj.*

salute, to keirei-suru *v.i. irr.*

same onaji *adj. & n-adj.*

sand suna *n.*

sandals zoori *n.* (39)

sash obi (belt) *n.*

satisfactory manzoku-na *n-adj.*

satisfied, be manzoku-suru *v.i. irr.*

Saturday Doyoobi *n.* (36)

save, to (to help) tasukeru *v.t. II.*

save, to (to store) tameru, takuwaeru *v.t. II.*, chochiku-suru *v.t. irr.*

saving chochiku, takuwae *n.*

say, to iu *v.i., v.t. I.* (38)

scale hakari (balance), uroko (of fish), memori (graduated marks), kibo (proportions) *n.*

scatter, to chiru *v.i. I.*; chirasu *v.t. I.*

school gakkoo *n.* (14)

science kagaku *n.*

scientific kagaku-teki-na *n-adj.*

scissors hasami *n.*

scold, to (to reprimand) shikaru *v.t. I.*

screw neji *n.*

sea umi *n.*

seashore kaigan, hama *n.*

seat seki *n.*

second (unit of time) byoo *n.* (35)

second tsugi-no, nibanme-no, *n-adj.* (33)

second day of the month futsuka (36)

secret himitsu *n.*

secret, keep himitsu-ni suru

see, to miru *v.t. II.* (18)

seed tane *n.*

self jibun, jishin *n.*

selfish rikoshugi-na, wagamama-na *n-adj.*

sell, to uru *v.t. I.*

send, to okuru *v.t. I.*

sentence bun, bunshoo *n.*

separate betsu-no *n-adj.*

separate, to wakeru *v.t. II.*, hanasu *v.t. I.*

separated hanareta (*adj.*)

September Kugatsu (36)

serene hogaraka-na *n-adj.*

serious majime-na (earnest), taihen-na *n-adj.*, omoi *adj.*

servant meshitsukai *n.*

serve, to (to wait upon) kyuuji-suru *v.t. irr.*, tsukaeru *v.i. II.*

set kumi *suf. & n.* (32)

set up, to tateru *v.t. II.*

seven nanatsu, shichi *n-adj.* (29, 30); seven days, seventh day nanuka (36)

sewerage gesui *n.*

shade (canopy) hiyoke *n.*

shadow kage *n.*

shake, to furu, yusuburu, furi-mawasu *v.t. I.*

shallow asai *adj.*

shame haji *n.*

shame, put to hazukashimeru ⌈*v.t.II.*

shape katachi *n.*

sharp surudoi *adj.*

shatter, to kudakeru *v.i. II.*, kudaku *v.t. I.*

shed, to (tears) nagasu *v.t. I.*

sheet mai *suf.* (31)

shelf tana *n.* (9)

shell fish kai *n.*

shine, to hikaru, kagayaku *v.i. I.*

ship fune *n.*

shirt shatsu (under shirt), wai-shatsu (white shirt) *n.* (6)

shoes kutsu *n.* (39)

shoot, to utsu *v.t. I.*

shop mise *n.*

short mijikai *adj.*

shorten, to chijimeru *v.t. II.*, chijimaru *v.i. I.*

shoulder kata *n.*

show, to miseru *v.t. II.*

shrink, to chijimu *v.i. I.*

shut, to shimeru *v.t. II.* (17), tojiru *v.t. II.*

sick, be kimochi-ga warui

sick, become byooki-ni naru

sickness byooki *n.*

sick person byoonin *n.*

side soba, waki, yoko *n.*

sidewise yoko-no *n-adj.*

silk kinu *n.*

shilkworm kaiko *n.*

silver gin *n.*

simple tanjun-na, kantan-na *⌊n-adj*

sin tsumi *n.*

since kara, yori *postp.* (19)

sincere makoto-no, majime-na *n-adj.*

sing, to utau *v.t. I.*

sink, to shizumu *v.i. I.*

sit, to (in a chair) kakeru, koshi-kakeru *v.i. II.* ⌈*I.* (18)

sit, to (on the floor) suwaru *v.i.*

six muttsu, roku *n-adj.* (29, 30) — days muika, —(cup) fuls roppai, — minutes roppun,

— "heads" roppiki, — pairs — sets mukumi, — "sticks" roppon (32, 36)

sixth day of the month muika (36)

size ookisa n.

skilful joozu-na n-adj., umai adj.

skill jukuren n.

skilled worker jukurenkoo n.

skin kawa, hifu n.

skirt hakama, sukaato n.

sky sora n.

sleep, to nemuru v.i. I., neru v.i. II.

sleeve sode n.

slide, to suberu v.i., v.t. I.

slip, to suberu v.i., v.t. I.

slow osoi, noroi adj.

small chiisai adj. (5)

smell nioi n.

smell, to niou v.i. I., kagu v.t. I.

smile, to nikoniko-suru v.i. irr., warau v.i. I.

smoke kemu, kemuri n.

smoke, to tabako-wo nomu

smokestack entotsu n.

smooth taira-na (6), namera-ka-na n-adj.

snake hebi n.

snow yuki n.

so soo adv. (3)

soap shabon, sekken n.

society shakai n.

soft yawarakai adj.

soil (earth) tsuchi, doro n.

soiled yogoreta (adj.), kitanai (dirty) adj.

soiled, be yogoreru v.i. II.

soldiers heitai, gunjin n.

solution eki, yooeki n.

solve, to toku v.t. I.

some ikuraka-no, ikutsuka-no, sukoshi-no n-adj. (44)

some (certain) aru (adj.)

somebody dareka

some other time itsuka

song uta n.

soon jiki-ni, mamonaku adv.

sore itai adj.

sorrow kanashimi n.

sorry kanashii adj.

sort (kind) shurui, rui n.

sound oto n.

south minami n.

speak, to hanasu v.i., v.t. I. (47)

special tokubetsu-no n-adj.

spectacles megane n.

speed hayasa, sokuryoku n.

spider kumo n.

spike kugi n.

spill, to kobosu, nagasu v.t. I.

spirit seishin, tamashii, genki (liveliness), yuurei (ghost) n.

spring haru (season) n.

spring (steel) bane n.

sprout me n.

stab, to tsuku, sasu v.t. I.

staircase dan, hashigo-dan n.

stalk kuki n. [(39)

stand, to tatsu v.i. I. (18)

standard hyoojun n.

standing screen tsuitate *n.* (39)

star hoshi *n.*

station, railway teishaba, eki *n.*

statue zoo *n.*

steal, to nusumu *v.t. I.*

steam jooki, yuge *n.*

steamer kisen *n.*

steel hagane, kootetsu *n.*

stem kuki, e *n.*

step (of a staircase) dan *n.* (39)

step on, to fumu *v.t. I.*

stick boo *n.*

stick, to tsuku *v.i. I.*, tsukeru *v.t. II.*

stillness shizukesa *n.*

stimulate, to shigeki-suru *v.t. irr.*

stimulus shigeki *n.*

stingy kechi-na *n-adj.*

stomach i *n.*

stomach (abdomen) hara *n.*

stone ishi *n.* (39)

stone lantern ishi-dooroo *n.*(54)

stop, to tomaru *v.i. I.*, tomeru *v.t. II.*

stop, to (to clog) fusagu *v.t. I.*

stop, to (give up) yameru *v.t. II.*

store (shop) mise *n.*

store (accumulation) takuwae *n.*

store, to takuwaeru, *v.t. II.*, chozoo-suru *v.t. irr.*

storehouse sooko, kura *n.*

storey kai *suf.* (52)

story hanashi *n.* (42, 51)

straight massugu-na *n-adj.*

straight line choku-sen *n.*

straw wara *n.*

strawberry ichigo *n.*

stream nagare *n.*

street machi, toori *n.* (52)

street car densha *n.* (21)

strength chikara, tsuyosa *n.*

stretch, to nobiru *v.i. II.*, nobasu *v.t. I.*

strict kibishii, katai *adj.*

strike, to utsu, butsu *v.t. I.*

string himo *n.*

strong tsuyoi *adj.* (46)

study benkyoo, kenkyuu *n.*

study, to benkyoo-suru, kenkyuu-suru *v.t. irr.*

style kata, shiki *n.*

subject (problem) dai, daimoku *n.*

subjugate, to shitagaeru *v.t. II.*

substitute kawari-no, daiyoo-no *n-adj.*

subway chika-tetsu (railway) chika-doo (road) *n.*

succeed, to seikoo-suru *v.i. irr.*

success seikoo *n.*

suck, to suu *v.t. I.*

sudden totsuzen-no *n-adj.*

suffer, to kurushimu *v.t. I.*

suffering kurushimi *n.*

sugar satoo *n.*

summer natsu *n.*

summit itadaki, choojoo *n.*

sun taiyoo, hi *n.*

Sunday Nichiyoobi *n.* (36)

sure tashika-na *n-adj.*

surely tashika-ni, kanarazu *adv.*

surprise, to odorokasu *v.t. I.*

surprised, be odoroku *v.i. I.*

surround, to kakomu *v.t. I.*

sweep, to haku *v.t. I.*

sweet (in taste) amai *adj.*

sweetness amasa *n.*

sweets (confectionary) o-kashi, kashi *n.* (44)

swell, to fukureru *v.i. II.*, fukuramu *v.i. I.*

swim, to oyogu *v.t. I.*

swing, to furu, furimawasu *v.t. I.*

sword katana *n.*

syllabary kana *n.* [*irr.*

sympathise, to doojoo-suru *v.i.*

sympathy doojoo *n.*

system soshiki *n.*

T

table dai, tsukue *n.* (15)

tack byoo *n.*

tag fuda *n.*

tail o, shippo *n.*

take, to toru *v.t. I.* (23, 24, 39)

take out, to dasu *v.t. I.*

talk hanashi *n.*

talk, to hanasu *v.t. I.*

tall takai, se no takai *adj.*

tame nareta (*adj.*)

tame, to narasu *v.t. I.*

tame, become nareru *v.i. II.*

taste aji (of food), konomi (liking) *n.*

taste, to ajiwau *v.t. I.*, aji-wo miru

tax zei *n.*

tea cha, o-cha *n.* (16)

tea cup yunomi *n.*

tea kettle (of earthen ware) dobin *n.* (26)

teach, to oshieru *v.t. II.* (38)

teacher sensei *n.* (49)

teaching (precept) oshie *n.*

tear namida *n.*

tear, to saku *v.t. I.*, sakeru *v.i. II.*

telegram denpoo *n.*

telegraph denshin *n.*

telephone denwa *n.*

telephone, to denwa-wo kakeru

tell, to hanasu *v.i. v.t. I.* (51)

temporary kari-no, ichiji-no *n-adj.*

ten too, juu *n-adj.*, (29, 30); — **days** tooka, —(cup) fuls jippai, — "**heads**" jippiki, — **minutes** jippun, — **pairs** — **sets** to-kumi, — **sen** jissen, — "**sticks**" jippon, — **volumes** jissatsu (32, 35)

tenth day of the month tooka (36)

ten thousand man, ichi-man *n-adj.* (30)

textile ori-mono *n.*

than yori *adv.* (34)

thank, to kansha-suru *v.t. irr.*

thank you arigatoo (27)

that sono, ano (*adj.*) (8); sore, are *pron.* (1)

theater gekijoo *n.*

there soko (9), asoko *pron.*

therefore kara, dakara *con.* (47)

thick atsui, futoi (big) *adj.*

thickness atsusa, futosa (bigness) *n.*

thief doroboo *n.*

thin usui (in thickness) *adj.*, yaseta (emaciated) (*adj.*)

thin, grow yaseru (emaciate *v.i. II.*

thing mono, shina *n.* (13)

think omou *v.i. v.t. I.* (42), kangaeru *v.i. v.t. II.*

third day of the month mikka (36)

this kore *pron.* (1), kono (*adj.*) (8)

this month kon-getsu (36)

this week kon-shuu (36)

this year kotoshi, kon-nen (36)

thought kangae *n.*

thousand sen, one thousand issen *n-adj.* (30)

thread ito *n.*

three mittsu, san *n-adj.* (28, 30); — days mikka, — (cup) fuls san-bai, — "heads" san-biki, — minutes san-pun, — pairs — sets mi-kumi, — "sticks" san-bon (32, 35, 36)

throat nodo *n.*

throw, to nageru *v.t. II.*, hooru

v.t. I.

throw away, to suteru *v.t. II.*

thunder kaminari, rai *n.*

Thursday Mokuyoobi *n.* (36)

ticket kippu *n.* (37)

tie, to musubu *v.t. I.*

till made *postp.*

till, to tagayasu *v.t. I.*

time toki (39), jikan *n.* (35)

time (as three times) do, hei su

tired tsukareta (*adj.*)

tired, be tsukareru *v.i. II.*

tired of, be (lose interest) akiru *v.i. II.*

to ni, e *postp.* (9, 27)

tobacco tabako *n.* (16)

tobacco tray tabako-bon *n.* (16)

today kyoo, kon-nichi (36)

together issho-ni *adv.*

tomorrow ashita, asu, myooni-chi *n.* (22, 36)

tongue shita *n.*

tool doogu *n.*

tooth ha *n.*

top ue, choojoo *n.* (11)

topple over, to taoreru *v.i. II.*

touch, to sawaru *v.i. I.*, fureru *v.i. II.*

town machi *n.* (52)

train (railway) kisha *n.* (50)

trample, to fumu *v.t. I.*, fumi-tsukeru *v.t. II.*

translate, to, honyaku-suru *v.t. irr.*

translation honyaku *n.*

travel tabi, ryokoo *n.*

travel, to tabi-suru, ryokoo-suru *v.i. irr.*

tray bon, sara (dish) *n.* (26)

tree ki *n.* (10, 39)

tremble, to furueru *v.i. II.*

trial kokoromi (experiment), saidan (judgement) *n.*

trouble mendoo *n.*

troubled, be komaru *v.i. I.* (49)

troublesome mendoo-na *n-adj.*

trousers zubon *n.*

try, to kokoromiru *v.t. II.*, yatte-miru *v.t. II.*, shi-te-miru *v.t. II.* (24)

tub oke, tarai *n.*

Tuesday Kayoobi *n.* (36)

turbid nigotta (*adj.*)

turbid, grow nigoru *v.i. I.*

turbidity nigori *n.*

turn (number) ban, junban *n.*

twentieth day of the month hatsuka (36)

twenty ni-juu *n-adj.* (30)

twenty days hatsuka (36)

twist, to nejiru *v.t. I.*

twisted, become nejireru *v.i. II.*

twisted nejireta *adj.*

two futatsu, ni *n-adj.* (28, 30) — days futsuka, — persons futari, — pairs — sets futakumi (32, 36)

type kata (style), katsuji (of printing) *n.*

U

ugly minikui, kitanai *adj.* (6)

umbrella kasa *n.*

uncle oji *n.*

under shita *n.*, -no shita-ni (11)

underground chika *n-adj.*

under-shirt shatsu *n.*

understand, to wakaru *v.i. I.*, rikai-suru *v.t. I.*

unit tan-i *n.*

university daigaku *n.* (54)

unreasonable muri-na *n-adj.*

untie, to hodokeru, tokeru *v.t. I.*

untied, become tokeru *v.i. II.*

until made (20)

upon -no ue-ni (11)

upside down sakasama-na *n-adj.*

use, to tsukau *v.t. I.* (37)

V

vacation yasumi, kyuuka *n.*

vague bonyari-shita (*adj.*)

vegetables yasai *n.*

vertical tate-no, suichoku-no *n-adj.*

very taihen, hijoo-ni *adv.* (14)

victory kachi, shoori *n.*

view (scene) nagame *n.*

view, to nagameru *v.t. II.*

village mura *n.*

virtue toku *n.*

voice koe *n.*

volume taiseki, yooseki *n.*

volume satsu *numeral adjunct* (31)

vomit, to haku *v.t. I.* ⌈*n-adj.*

vulgar iyashii *adj.*, katoo-na

W

wait, to matsu *v.t. I.*

wait on, to kyuuji-suru *v. i. irr.*

waiter kyuuji, booi *n.*

wake up, to okiru *v.i. II.*, me-wo samasu, okosu *v.t. I.* (24)

wall kabe *n.* (16, 54)

want, to -tai *aux. v.* (52), hoshii *adj.* (52), hoshigaru *v.t. I.*

war sensoo *n.*

warm atatakai *adj.*

warmth atatakasa *n.*

warrior doll musha ningyoo *n.* (46)

wash, to arau *v.t. I.*, sentaku-suru *v.t. irr.*

watch (timepiece) tokei *n.*

watch, to chuui-suru, mihari-suru *v.t. irr.*

water mizu *n.* (21)

water-closet benjo, habakari *n.*

water tap suidoo-sen *n.*

water works suidoo *n.*

wave nami *n.*

weak yowai *adj.*

wear, to kiru (on body) *v.t. II.*, kaburu (on head) *v.t. I.*, haku (on feet) *v.t. I.* (39)

wear out, to suri-kireru *v.i. II.*

weather tenki *n.*

weave, to oru *v.t. I.*

Wednesday Suiyoobi *n.* (36)

weed kusa, zassoo *n.*

week shuukan *n.* (36)

weep, to naku, susuri-naku

v.i. I.

weigh, to hakaru *v.t. I.*

weight omosa *n.*

welcome kangei *n.*

well ido *n.*

well yoku *adv.*

west nishi *n.*

wet nureta, shimetta (*adj.*)

wet, become nureru *v.i. II.*

what? nani, nan *pron. & (adj.* (2)

what day of the month? nan-nichi, what day of the week? nani-yoobi, what month? nan-gatsu, what time? nan-ji (35, 36) what kind of don-na (5)

wheat mugi *n.*

wheel kuruma, sharin *n.*

when? itsu *pron. & adv.* (19)

where? doko, dochira *pron.* (9)

which? dore (which one among many), dochira (which one of the two) *pron.*; dono (among many), dochira-no (of the two) *adj.* (33, 34)

while aida-ni *adj.*, nagara *suf.*

whip muchi *n.*

white shiro *n.*, shiroi *adj.*

who? donata, dare *pron.* (4)

wide hiroi *adj.* (7)

width hirosa, haba *n.*

wife fujin, tsuma, oku-san *n.* (39)

will power ishi *n.*

win, to katsu *v.i. I.*

wind kaze *n.*

wind, to maku *v.t. I.*

window mado *n.* (15)

wine sake *n.*

winter fuyu *n.*

wipe, to fuku, nuguu *v.t. I.*

wire harigane *n.*

wise rikoo-na *n-adj.* (13), kashi-koi *adj.*

wish, negai, nozomi *n.*

wish, to negau, nozomu *v.t. I.*

with de *postp.*, wo motte

woman onna, onna-no hito *n.* (42)

wood ki *n.* (10, 39); wooden ki-no *n-adj.*

wooden clog geta *n.* (35)

word kotoba *n.*

work shigoto, tsutome, yoo *n.*

work, to hataraku *v.i. I.*, tsutomeru *v.i. II.* shigoto-wo suru

world sekai *n.*

worm mushi *n.* (10)

worry shinpai *n.*

worry, to shinpai-suru *v.t. irr.*

wound kega *n.*

wounded, be kega-suru *v.i. irr.*

wrap , to tsutsumu *v.t. I.*

wrapping paper tsutsumi-gami *n.*

wrestle, to sumoo-wo toru

wrestling sumoo *n.*

write, to kaku *v.t. I.* (23)

writing brush fude *n.*

Y

yard niwa *n.* (10)

year toshi *n.*, nen *suf.* (36)

years old -sai *suf.* (36)

yell, to donaru, sakebu *v.t. I.*

yellow kiiro *n.*, kiiroi *adj.*

yes hai *interj.* (2)

yesterday kinoo, sakujitsu *n.* (19, 36)

yet mada *adv.* (43)

you anata, kimi (used by young men), omae (used toward inferior persons) *pron.* (2)

young wakai *adj.*

younger brother otooto *n.*

younger sister imooto *n.*

Z

zero rei *n.* (30)

zoological garden doobutsu-en *n.*

hon, shomotsu — book
empitsū — pencil
pen — pen (Jap.brush) fude
Kami — paper
Stop! (tomaru) to stop tomete!
migi — Right
hidari — left